A CURIOUS EYE

Observations of a psychotherapist

Patricia Gosling

*

WHITE HART BOOKS

Printed on acid free paper

British Library Cataloguing In Publication Data

A Record of this Publication is available
from the British Library

ISBN 1846853516
978-1-84685-351-7

First Edition 2006
Second printing 2006
Published by White Hart Books
at the White Hart, Rode, England
In association with Exposure Publishing
an imprint of Diggory Press
Three Rivers, Minions, Liskeard, Cornwall, PL14 5LE, UK
WWW.DIGGORYPRESS.COM

Dedication

*

To my favourite people — in gratitude for all that they have given me.

For my family and friends,
who must often have wondered what I got up to in my
professional life.

For my colleagues,
who will be more aware of the subtleties and deficiencies revealed
here.

As psychotherapists we need forgiveness more than most!

———————————

Contents

Acknowledgments

'VE-Day and After' first appeared in *Viewpoint*, the journal of the Guild of Psychotherapists which was produced and edited for some years by Ann Orbach. Sadly the journal did not long survive her retirement from the post.

Many short pieces that follow appeared in *The Newsletter*, later *Bulletin and Review* and subsequently *50 Minutes*, the journal of the Severnside Institute for Psychotherapy, which the author edited from 1990 to 2000. She is grateful to those colleagues who successively held the Chair of SIP during this period, Herbert Hahn, Paul Zeal and Muriel Mitcheson Brown, for the support and freedom they gave her in this task. Some of these pieces are slight and very much 'of the moment', but they reflect the preoccupations of the author at that time.

The paper 'The Blind Men and the Elephant' was given as part of a symposium on *Eclecticism* at a Severnside Institute Study Weekend held in June, 1990 at the Postgraduate Centre, Frenchay Hospital, Bristol.

The paper 'The Cannibal Gods' was first given at a Members' Meeting of the SIP in July, 1997 at 11 Orchard Street, Bristol.

'What is Human?' and 'The Imprint of God' came out of a long-term relationship with the Clinical Theology Association, a pastoral counselling organisation founded in 1962 by the psychiatrist and Anglican priest Frank Lake whose avowed aim was to integrate the languages of psychotherapy and religion. 'What is Human?' was given as the key-note speech at the Annual CTA Conference in 1994 at the University of Keele. 'The Imprint of God' was given as the 1998 Frank Lake Memorial Lecture in Oxford. The author is immensely grateful to Peter van de Kasteele, the then Director of

CTA, who issued both invitations to speak, not least for his faith in her untried capacity.

My profound thanks to William Gosling who, in the face of a considerable lack of enthusiasm, has managed to impart to me some basic computer skills.

He has also survived many years in the exacting role of psychotherapist's spouse, and only those within the profession will know just how much patience and perseverance that has demanded.

I should like to express my appreciation, also, to those of my former patients who were generous enough to permit me to use clinical material derived from our work together.

Last but not least, I must record my indebtedness to Martin Miller and Dr. Harold Stewart of the British Psychoanalytical Society who embodied for me enduring examples of how to be both professional and compassionate.

Needless to say, the opinions and perspectives that follow are entirely my own.

Introduction

The word 'curious' is used here in both its senses.

Psychotherapists are, and must be, in order to practice their profession, insatiably curious about people and what makes them tick. It is a curiosity acquired, I suspect, very early in life; from days spent lying in a cot struggling to understand the world, and the people in it. Perhaps for some fortunate infants this world is so orderly and predictable that they can readily make sense of it, take that sense for granted and build creatively upon it. For others, that world is so hopelessly chaotic that they give up the struggle for meaning and go on to live lives that either mirror that chaos, or that achieve stability at the expense of being psychically impoverished. Another group withdraw much of their emotional investment in people, find their meaning in the non-human environment, and hope in the material world.

For the infant psychotherapist, people are puzzling but fascinating. The sense they offer is elusive but there is always the hope and expectation that sense can be found. The profession of psychotherapist is, I suggest, an extension into adult life of a pattern which has long become compulsive.

This profession, like all professions, leaves its mark on its practitioners. They do not see the world in quite the same way as other groups of people. While they differ (often vociferously) amongst themselves, nonetheless they share certain ways of seeing the world which may appear eccentric to others. In that sense also they have a curious eye.

The following essays are the spontaneous comments of one particular therapist.

On re-reading them, certain recurring preoccupations become apparent. In common with many of my colleagues, I have found that patients increasingly present as borderline personalities or with problems of narcissism. I cannot be sure whether this represents a real change in the patient population, or whether we have changed our ways of looking at and conceptualising the phenomena we meet. I suspect both are true. Certainly our society not only sanctions the rampant individualism and self-absorption of the narcissistic personality, but positively encourages it through the values, attitudes and cultural icons promoted by the media.

Another recurrent theme, expressed at various levels, is that of living with and integrating difference. In my training with the Guild of Psychotherapists, (1979-83) I was exposed to (and chose) an eclectic training. Subsequently, the Severnside Institute for Psychotherapy was created (1985) with a deliberately eclectic ethos. Inevitably, this made for tensions and uncertainties which had to be struggled with at organisational and inter-personal levels, as well as confusion for the student. If I found it less difficult than many, I can only think that it arose from my experience of growing up in a mixed Welsh/English family which contained within it two very different perspectives on life. The work of observing, thinking about, sifting and testing which this demanded was second nature to me long before I had reached adulthood. It probably helped too that I had acquired a settled theoretical perspective within the Independent Freudian tradition before I began my formal training. The broad theoretical church that this tradition represents allowed me to consider, welcome and make use of ideas from other traditions when they had the pragmatic sanction.

The downside of this position is that one never fully belongs, that one is always something of an outsider, living on the border. I suspect that is true of many of my fellow professionals. I suspect too that it makes us better as psychotherapists if at the expense of our personal comfort.

The need to integrate different perspectives has surfaced during professional discussions of multi-cultural issues, and is overt in my two papers 'What is Human?' and 'The Imprint of God.' I have long seen psychotherapy and religion as two attempts, one very ancient, one more recent, to address and make sense of the human condition in all its miseries and glories. To see them as irreparably at odds is foolish; the possibilities of creative cross-fertilisation are immense and much needed.

I believe it would help us manage and understand our differences if we were more willing to acknowledge the extent to which our own personal and cultural history had formed our individual belief systems. The claim to theoretical infallibility which has dogged the history of psychoanalysis as much as that of the Church smacks to my mind of infantile omniscience. The moral of the story 'The Blind Men and the Elephant' remains highly relevant.

Although as psychotherapists we spend many hours cocooned in our consulting rooms absorbed in matters of the inner psychic world, nonetheless like everyone else we still have to live our lives within the wider environment, which brings its own limits, demands and impingements. It also faces us with values and attitudes often at odds with those central to our professional concerns. Here too we all of us have the task of trying to integrate the various bits of our lives, including life within the family if we are fortunate enough to have one.

This book comes out of the struggle of one individual in that ongoing task of how to be both professional and human.

Rode

(2006)

10

The Analytic Hour

The silence is tangible, dense.
I drop a word into the pool and watch the ripple.
She replies in kind.
The silence broods.

Another word—a flurry, a sudden gust.
Thunderclouds loom.
Then—she erupts. The storm breaks,
The fury is let loose.
I sit at the eye of the hurricane as all Hell whirls round.

At last, slowly, the maelstrom subsides.
The sun comes out, a blissful calm descends.
She smiles through the tears.
How amazing!
I had forgotten how bad it was—that it all hurt so much.
How very odd!

Reluctantly, our time is up.
We go through the ritual of parting -
The small sad smile, the lingering backward glance.
It was a good session, we did some useful work.
Till tomorrow, then.

(1996)

Sounding-off
The Theory Applied

*

VE-Day* and After

The VE-day celebration stirred my memories, inevitably, but they were past, not present ones. I was lucky! Wartime life, for me, if bleak and boring, was more or less normal. If the bombers droned overhead every night, they dumped their bombs elsewhere. The cocoon of childhood was not shattered.

A few things linger. The sound of a propeller-driven aircraft still makes me uneasy, a dying siren sets my teeth on edge. I recall the first photographs out of Belsen; they were printed on a certain quality of shiny paper; the smell of it still makes me retch. I learned the knack of rolling out of my warm bed, down into the cellar and into a makeshift bunk without properly waking up. It stood me in good stead later when I worked as a medical student on the maternity wards, and again when I had my own young!

I inherited my mother's hamster instincts. Her thrifty hoarding habits did much to moderate the meagre rations and intermittent shortages of those years, and my own store cupboards are still unnecessarily full against disaster. Innumerable reels of Movietone News with their stirring, hearty commentaries bred in me a fierce pacifism which has modified only as my own analysis put me in touch with the murderous anger within me! For years, I could never become anxious, though I appropriately should have done so —the expected disaster never did arrive.

If the war coloured my young life, it did not distort it. However, I am surprised how often in my consulting room, I find I am still dealing with the long-term effects of those days.

A middle-aged man had been evacuated, aged seven, by train, and without his parents. They had later joined him, but he had never gone back home. That home disappeared in the Blitz, as did his cat, his closest friend and their next-door neighbours. He still found it difficult ever to go away on holiday, and was surprised, at the end of a day's work, to find his wife and home where he had left them that morning. He had nightmares about conflagrations, and phobic panics when travelling by train. He tried hard not to get too attached, would cheerfully abandon all his possessions; and phases of close intimacy were cyclically followed by phases of schizoid withdrawal. He was plagued by a fear of death—the loss ahead as certain as the loss behind. To the outside world he was successful and creative, if sometimes hypomanic. He was driven by anxiety.

A woman of similar age had also suffered evacuation, though eventually returning to her original home. Because of the nature of her parents' work, they had flitted, sometimes together, sometimes separated, from one place to another. After a couple of years, and nine changes of school, she was eventually left with an aunt in the country. She was able to recall how, at this point, she 'cut off' from her parents and the threatening world 'out there', and retreated, apparently happy and content, into a 'children's world' with her beloved cousin.

When I met her she was still estranged from and obscurely angry with her mother, intensely ambivalent towards her father, with her warmest feelings reserved for her aunt. Throughout her life, she had 'flitted' from one enthusiasm and activity to another, never staying with any one thing long enough for real achievement in spite of intelligence and ability. She still 'cut off' from anything painful or anything she did not want to see. In some areas she could not/would not see what was under her nose. It left her selectively naive, and unable to use experience. She married a man with the name and temperament of her cousin. The normal separations of therapy led to destructive acting-out which proved

16

hard to contain, and she taught me more about the different varieties of resistance than any patient I can recall!

A man in his thirties, successful in his profession, was two years old when his father returned from the war, and imploded into his small world. Unfortunately, he had been recently hospitalised for a tonsillectomy, had felt abandoned by his mother (no mothers living-in in those days!), and had had no time to work through that experience before all the rules of his established world changed. His father felt that he was being 'spoiled' by his mother, and instilled some 'discipline' into the system. Small wonder that in many areas of his life he felt and behaved as if castrated. He seemed to attract persecutory people, and the most minor illness devastated him.

An intelligent and able woman was three when her father returned from a POW camp. His appearance marked the end of her doomed attempt to establish the relationship she needed with her mother. Beforehand, her elder sister had held the centre of the stage; afterwards, her father monopolised it. Part of his reinstatement as head of the household was to take over the children's discipline. His response to any naughtiness in her was to 'thrash the living daylights' out of her.

During therapy she became more deeply aware of her unconscious assumption that all men are profoundly insensitive; do not feel as women do; do not experience emotional hurt; are immune to the feelings of those around them; and are bullies given half a chance. Intellectually, she knew this was nonsense—she was fortunate to have married an above-averagely sensitive, intuitive (and patient!) man, and she 'knew' her son was quite as easily hurt as his sisters —but she had never integrated the two areas of her experience. Her attractive personality was often disrupted by the compulsive need to be provocatively naughty. Underlying was a disintegrating level of pain, a chronic desire for 'out', and a feeling of worthlessness which would have astonished her acquaintances and work-mates.

N. never knew the war. She was born soon afterwards to parents who had survived the German army of occupation in Europe, and the Allies' bombardment. They had been separated for much of this

17

time, the father in the army, the mother moving around, from place to place, from relative to friend, and nearly losing her life in the final invasion. N. knew that at some time they had armed themselves with 'suicide pills' in case life became intolerable.

A part of N.'s complaint against her mother was the manner in which, during her childhood, people, pets and possessions disappeared. The family dog, and her own hamster, vanished without warning while she was away from home. Familiar possessions, her bedroom chair, were thrown out without consultation—'You don't need those old things any more!' (She has to take care that she does not do the same to her own children, so she knows the memory is real!)

Her parents would go on holiday leaving her with neighbours, or in a children's holiday camp, with minimal preparation for the break, and without checking, before or afterwards, whether she was comfortable with the arrangement. It was all done in such a way that she felt unable to complain.

She did not know where they had gone or how to get in touch with them. She received only the odd, brief postcard, and never felt sure that they would ever come back to find her. Later on, they would leave the children at home during their holiday with a sealed envelope in a locked drawer and instructions what to do with it 'if anything should happen to us'.

Also, it was as if N.'s mother had her own fantasy of how life ought to be, and was inconsolably angry with everybody and everything that it wasn't so. From without, family life looked good, from within it felt unbearable, and N. felt damaged by it all. No wonder she. felt 'wrong'.

We had talked about these things many times before in terms of family dynamics, and the anger that lay between N. and her mother. It was only the VE-day anniversary that prompted us to talk again about the family's wartime experience, and to reveal a pattern we had previously missed. The father had been heard to say that his wife 'was never the same woman' after her near-death experience. It was as if she had never come to terms with all that

she had gone through, and continued to act it out—the sudden
flights from one place to another, the lack of preparation, the
separations to be endured without fuss, the necessity for stoic
endurance at all times, the unimportance of personal property, the
denial, the refusal to see others' hurt, the interminable complaints
—'It didn't ought to be like this!' and 'I need someone to look after
me!'

It seemed to be part of the pattern that N. took flight to a foreign
country to escape the annihilating pain of home; that both parents
died with almost no warning within a few weeks of each other; and
that the mother took steps to cut short her dying process. The
feeling that 'It shouldn't have happened like that!' has passed on to
the next generation.

Many families suffered in the war far more than these. It could be
argued, justly, that these people were already vulnerable because of
the family dynamics at work before these events took place. I am
impressed by the strengths which enabled them to come through as
well as they have.

The war may have come to an end forty years ago. I cannot but feel
that the casualty list is still incomplete.

*VE-day – Victory in Europe Day: the anniversary of the signing of the
treaty in May, 1945 which brought to an end the war in Europe.*

(1985)

The Singer and the Song

Many years ago, I spent a term alongside another faculty wife and a gaggle of hairy M.Sc. students—and in those days (the 60s) students were quite remarkably hirsute!—learning how to programme a computer. The rationale behind this unlikely activity now escapes me. I can only think it was a case of 'if you can't beat 'em, join 'em', since most of my adult contacts at that time were talking incessant, enthusiastic and, to me, meaningless jargon about these amazing bits of technology.

Sadly, my own enthusiasm never rose above lukewarm, and I soon forgot what little I had learned. However, some impressions have remained indelibly in my mind.

I soon decided that this particular form of 'intelligence' was actually quite stupid. For instance, it did exactly what you told it to do, however nonsensical. Even my old dog had more sense than that! Secondly, although it was very good at doing things people were bad at because they found them so boring, such as adding up long columns of sums very quickly, it was poor at other tasks where people excel, such as pattern recognition. Since much of our work as psychotherapists is concerned with recognising patterns of human thought and feeling, I think our jobs are safe from a takeover bid!

I learned, too, that provided one is not frightened of these machines and instructs them clearly and firmly what to do, they can be quite remarkably versatile. It was, I recall, the Christmas term, and the aforesaid students spent several weeks churning out an impressive array of Christmas cards and calendars varying from the mildly pornographic (par for the age-group!) to the touchingly artistic.

Those fluent in the management of these machines swore that they had personalities, and that these personalities at times became disturbed. This I could believe both from the devotion they engendered, and the behaviour of their operators when they became disordered. The countertransference behaviour evoked had a distinctly manic-depressive quality, swinging from profound depressive apathy to prolonged, frenzied, sleep-denying activity which no sensible reasoning could pierce. While actual violence was rare, threats were frequent and daunting!

Above all, I learned to distinguish between 'hardware' and 'software'.

To those still innocently unfamiliar with the jargon, 'hardware' is the physical structure—the mechanical/electronic bits and pieces which one can handle and see, although one may have to use a microscope in order to do the seeing. 'Software' is the programming—the complicated data and instructions given to the machine which provides its 'intelligence' and its particular 'personality', and the capacity to perform all the complex activities we demand from it. The corollary of this is that two machines may have identical hardware, but very different software, and hence be experienced as quite different machines in terms of behaviour.

I find this hardware/software distinction a very useful concept in thinking about our own work, and feel that a wider understanding of it would put an end to much tedious and unsatisfying wrangling between ourselves and others.

It seems to me that what, as psychotherapists, we are concerned with is the human software, the programming that we have received during our formative years. Our work is aimed at modifying that software to make it more compatible with objective external reality, and with itself. I say 'with itself' because I see a lot of symptomatology as the result of mutually incompatible bits of programming, leaving the person attempting to solve inherently insoluble problems. In 'objective external reality' I would include the social norms and expectations of the individual's culture, but also a realistic appraisal of our own hardware and its innate limitations.

Of course, some of our software comes built-in—what in the jargon is known as 'firmware'—a part of the psyche-soma. This is our genetic endowment, natural instincts, innate disposition, and I think we have to accept it as given and unchangeable. Other bits of programming occur so early, during intra-uterine life, while undergoing the experience of birth, or in the post-partum period, that I suspect they too have to be regarded as firmware, and probably not susceptible to change. Any modification of our programming seems to be accompanied by pain, and the earlier the programming, the greater the pain. The changes that come easily are probably of little significance; would that it were not so!

You may feel that this is very crude way of understanding the human psyche in view of the immense subtleties and complexities that are our everyday fare in the consulting-room. It is; but I do not think it in any way contradicts or undermines psychodynamic theory as we understand it.

It is, I suggest, a perspective which cuts through much of the interminable argument and confusing verbiage which all too often sets in when members of our profession attempt discussion with those from other backgrounds and disciplines.

The medical profession, for example, has been generally unsympathetic to our approach because its obsessive concern is with the human hardware. The techniques which have paid such handsome dividends in treating hardware defects have been less than satisfactory in tackling essentially software problems.

The two professions, medical and psychotherapeutic, need to develop a common viewpoint if we are ever to understand and satisfactorily treat those interesting conditions where both hardware and software faults are at work. People differ from computers in that our hardware, being organic, is in a state of constant change. Growth, renewal and degeneration are always at work in varying proportions.

We have understood for a long time that hardware faults can affect our software; obvious examples are Alzheimer's disease, tertiary syphilis, a high fever. We increasingly suspect that severe and prolonged software dysfunction can interfere with basic hardware processes. Here we are into that fascinating area that is psychosomatic medicine—peptic ulcer, hypertension, thyrotoxicosis, rheumatoid arthritis, many skin complaints. The more we learn, the longer grows the list of designated auto-immune diseases when the body turns against itself; and we all know that our susceptibility to the common cold varies with our emotional well-being.

I wonder, too, about schizophrenia. Is the vulnerability to it truly inherited with the genetic package, or is it a firmware defect as the result of severe, early stressing? Perhaps it can be either, or both.

One result of looking at human process in these terms is that it puts an end to that tiresome argument, is psychoanalysis a science or is it not. Given his own training and the fashionable intellectual ideas of his time, it was an understandable aspiration of Freud's that his talking cure should be accepted as scientific. It was, however, a misguided aspiration. In terms of the mechanistic/ reductionist science of his day, it is difficult to believe that psychoanalytical treatment could ever meet the criteria of proof demanded. I feel that his attempts to argue the case distorted the development of his models and language, and the overall result was negative.

However, being the great man he undoubtedly was, he was typical in being ahead of his time. Although we still tend to be taught our science at school in the old terms, it has in fact moved on. From the understanding of thermodynamics through control, system and automata theory to communication theory and artificial intelligence, a whole, new, holistic way of thinking about the physical world has developed. Few would still argue that these disciplines are unscientific, (although some are not altogether comfortable with them!) It terms of this way of thinking, there is no problem in seeing psychoanalysis as scientific.

I expect we have all at times tried to explain what we psychotherapists do to others quite outside our speciality, and found it a near-impossible task. I know I have largely given up trying. However, next time you find yourself in the company of engineers or similar others, try introducing yourself as a human software engineer and watch the light of comprehension steal across the features.

Incidentally, for those whose thinking includes a theological dimension, the concept of human software gives scientific respectability at long last to the notion of a soul!

To sum up, an aphorism from an unknown source:-

> The difference between hardware and software is
>
> the difference between the singer and his song.

Our work is with the song.

(1989)

The Geometry of Nature

Earlier this year, I was privileged to hear a lecture given by Benoit Mandelbrot. If you can't quite place that name, he is the originator of the theory of fractals which is provoking so much interest in scientific circles. In the flesh, he is a large genial teddy-bear of a man with a rapid Isaiah Berlin-type delivery and a pronounced Franco-Swiss accent, which did not augur well for my concentration at the end of a long, working day. However, this was an experienced teacher, and the combination of a delightful sense of humour, a deceptively simple manner and a clear, direct line of thought soon dispelled any misgivings.

He began by showing a short sequence of slides; and these encapsulated his basic argument. The first was of a large modern building, International style, all straight lines and square angles, lots of plate glass and not a trace of ornamentation. To one side of the foreground, framing the building, was a tree, with its irregular tracery of branches and leaves. This visual image symbolised the first point in his exposition.

Mandelbrot went on to explain that he saw his mathematical formulations as the geometry of living things, in contrast to Euclidian geometry—the kind that we struggled with at school, and which is what most of us think of as 'geometry'. Indeed, if Mandelbrot's equations are mapped out in visual form—and some of you may have seen his 'pictures'—what emerges is something that looks like a part of the living world. To me, they are somewhere between a complicated Paisley pattern, an elaborate bit of seaweed marquetry of the kind beloved by the 17th century Dutch cabinet-makers, or a map of a highly-indented, rocky

25

coastline; and they are curiously beautiful. What is surprising is that these highly elaborate patterns are an expression of relatively simple formulae; and one can begin to believe that many apparently complex natural phenomena have an underlying simplicity of structure.

Where does that leave our old kind of geometry? Mandelbrot would see it now as a special case, perfectly valid within certain limits of operation, but essentially limited in its application— enabling us to build Bauhaus-type buildings, but of no help in understanding the natural world.

He next showed us a slide of two almost identical pictures. The first was a magnified cross-section of a spadeful of earth. One could see the striated levels as one moved down from the friable top-soil to the compacted sub-soil. The second picture looked like another spadeful of earth from another bit of the garden. It was only when he showed us a third slide—a repeat of the second, but with a man in the picture to give us a sense of scale—that we realised we were looking at a cliff-face of several hundred feet drop.

This was a neat and telling way of illustrating an important point, namely that the patterns his formulae express can be found in nature at all levels of magnification. Indeed, if one takes one of the Mandelbrot patterns and magnifies a small portion of it, hoping to see the 'rocky indentations' more clearly, what is revealed is another 'coastline' with just as much detail in it; and one can go on repeating this ad infinitum. The underlying pattern is the same, and there is no end to it.

As the lecture moved into the realm of mathematical formulation, my concentration began to drift back to the day's work and my own preoccupations. I wondered if there was something here that was applicable to our own professional concerns.

It seems to me that we are all of us, whether original thinkers or devoted followers, all too apt to see our own particular metapsychology as a complete theory, when it is actually, like Euclid's geometry, a special case in a more general theory that we do not yet have. This is not to belittle any particular set of ideas—after all, Euclid's geometry has served us well for a long time, and one can understand the fury of those who have built their life's work and professional reputation on elaborating concepts within this framework, when confronted with such new ideas. Galileo had a rough time, too, when he upset the intellectual apple-cart of his day!

I wonder, too, if there is something we can use in the concept of the same patterning operating at different levels of magnification, so to speak. How much are the differences between the various schools of thought caused by the different level of experience to which we address ourselves? Could one make a case, for example, for seeing the Zurich Jungians, with their developed understanding of ancient myths and primitive archetypes, operating at the cliff-face level, while others were examining their everyday spit of earth, and others still were peering down their microscopes. Could one even make a case in all this for astrology—an area that I know intellectually is scientific nonsense, but which is so often uncannily accurate in its predictions. (Well, as I have said, it was getting late and I was feeling the need for a decent meal, and my fantasies were getting dangerously close to dreaming!)

I realised, as I drove home, that I was still struggling with the issues of eclecticism, and the need for finding a way of thinking that will allow us the freedom of our own hard-won understanding, while maintaining respect for those who have a different perspective. The same kind of argument could perhaps be used to illuminate the issues around multi-culturalism, which was one of the preoccupations of our recent study weekend; but that is a thorny tangle which demands its own separate space.

(1991)

Outer World / Inner World

A patient was wondering if the world was currently more troubled than usual. Given recent events in the Gulf, the unrest in the Soviet Union, and the changes on the face of Europe during the last year or so, this was a not unreasonable comment.

However, it had particular significance for my patient, since the stability of her inner world is constantly threatened by a sense of impending chaos and confusion. For the most part she manages her life very well by organising it into discrete 'bites' separated by enough space in which she can think through what is happening to her. This on-going continual work readily becomes threatened if she becomes too busy or tired, or external events impinge in an unmanageable way. She rapidly becomes quite distressed, and is flooded by feelings of meaninglessness. Life is then a matter of stoical survival on what she describes as her 'bomb site'.

The war analogy is apt, for her life has been indelibly marked and marred by the impact of the '39-'45 conflict upon her infancy. The disappearance of her father at a crucial phase of her development, the loss of her first home, moving from place to place, all this must

28

have been utterly bewildering to a toddler who had not yet achieved object constancy. After a year or more of such disruption, a new home was found within the extended family, at which point the mother vanished for another year. It was as if every time my patient managed to make some sense of her daily life, the pattern was shattered, until it hardly seemed worth making the effort.

All this would have been hard for any child, but less so if there had been a mother around who could provide some basic framework of meaning and routine, some continuity and consistency, who could act as a shield against impingement. Sadly, this mother was herself inconsistent, impulsive and impinging. The infant's relationship with her had already been shattered over and over again before external events conspired to reproduce the pattern.

Inevitably, in the transference I have been experienced as negligent, uncaring, emotionally absent, not-good-enough, inadequately protective and clumsy. Nowadays I find I must be more verbally active than is my wont as I make links for her, identify analogies and give meaning to what she experiences as senseless, pointless and without meaning. It has taken me a long time to appreciate the necessity to do this for someone who outside the therapeutic relationship is astute, insightful and highly intelligent.

In this session, there seemed to be for both of us some analogy between the inner experience of stability being repeatedly shattered, and the television scenes we have both witnessed in recent days—the massive destruction in both Kuwait City and Baghdad, the disappearance of architectural landmarks, the devastation of the infra-structure of civilised life—water, power, telecommunications, the Armageddon of that last convoy out of Kuwait, the disintegration of the belief system purveyed by a dishonoured Sadam Hussein to the Iraqi people. The confusion and bewilderment in the eyes of the Iraqi soldiers, in the face of a returned British P.O.W., in a stunned and horrified journalist, seemed echoes of something she knew only too well, the unwelcome confirmation of an inner reality.

For the damaged child, for the traumatised war casualties, for the shattered country, there would seem to be a primary need, above all else, for some envelope of safety, some framework of meaning without which life is experienced as fragmented, pointless and unbearable.

(1991)

[This piece was written at the time of the first Gulf War. Iraqi forces had invaded Kuwait in an attempt to annexe that Emirate. This led to retaliation by armed forces of the UK and USA and a total rout of the original attackers.]

Some Random Thoughts About Babies

A new baby has recently arrived in the family, so I have been able to carry out some surreptitious baby observation. Since this is a first baby, proud father has been clicking his camera at every opportunity, whilst the female members of the clan vie ever-so-politely for the opportunity to cuddle this latest addition to their ranks. Looking through the first batch of photographs covering 0 - 21 days, I notice something of which I have never previously been aware. Whoever is holding this infant, the expression on its face mirrors that of the nursing adult. This is particularly marked between mother and child, but it is clearly there with others too. Dad has a sequence to himself which passes from benign curiosity through anxiety to frustration and rage, but he is not at all sure who is teaching whom in this process of mutual education! What is apparent to me is that this infant is already doing its best to become an acceptable member of this particular family by adopting the facial expressions of the receiving group.

It should not surprise me. We have all, probably, met adopted children who closely resemble their adoptive parents. I have friends whose grandson bears a powerful resemblance to his grandfather. It was only when I commented on this resemblance that I learned that there is in fact no blood tie between them, since the mother was adopted. (I can only speculate that her choice of

31

husband was influenced by his resemblance to her father.) And we all laugh at the way dogs come to look like their owners; or do we choose dogs whose faces remind us of our own?

I recall how, during my training as a psychotherapist, I attended some seminars given by Christopher Bollas, and heard him talk, very persuasively, about the mutual cueing that goes on between babies and their mothers. This was the first time I had come across this phrase, and I thought it a very deft description of the way children bring up their parents, and vice versa.

I was reminded of this as I listened to a radio programme recently, *Medicine Now: June 18th, 1991*. A report from a conference on nutrition contained some material I found fascinating. Apparently there is considerable evidence coming forward which suggests that the nutrition offered during the earliest days and weeks of life, and possibly during intra-uterine life too, conditions the physiological responses of the rest of that individual's life. It seems that the infant takes note, at some level, of such factors as how plentiful food is, the variety of different nutriments on offer, the relative proportions of the various ingredients etc., and builds the information so gained into its physiological expectations. The nutritionist reporting on this, still experimental, evidence pointed out how this adaptive response makes for survival of the infant. It is the way the infant adapts to the conditions of life in which it finds itself. For example, if food is in short supply, it has a mechanism for learning to use it to best advantage; it can then extract what it needs from what is on offer. Once learned, this information apparently becomes an indelible part of the individual's firmware; and one can immediately see that here we have a basis for understanding certain conditions, emerging later in life, where matters have clearly gone awry; for example, intractable obesity, and possibly other metabolic disorders.

It does suggest that, from the very beginning of extra-uterine life if not earlier, the infant is learning how to become a member of the particular community, the particular family, into which it is born. Like it or not, that is where we are rooted, in the physiological as much as the psychological sense.

Time and further research will confirm or deny these tentative findings. What seems undeniable is the incredible capacity of the human infant to learn, and to adapt to the world into which it is born. What seems equally certain is the extreme difficulty of modifying that early learning. All this, of course, long before the acquisition of language, before those words which are the coinage of our psychotherapeutic technique; and before memory of the kind normally available to recall.

However, we do have means of communication other than words. We receive, and transmit, a great deal of information by means of, for example, body language—posture, gait, facial expression; manner of dress; the use of space and time; the use of the artefacts in our environment; the environment we create around us in home and work-place. These factors are not strictly part of therapy, but many of them enter into the therapeutic encounter, and provide us with clues about the inner world and the earliest experience of the outer world.

Christopher Bollas has some interesting things to say in his book *The Shadow of the Object*: ch. 6. 'Moods and the conservative process'. He writes about the way information is encapsulated within a mood. At times in an ongoing therapy, a certain mood will creep into the relationship which may have little apparent connection with what has ostensibly been happening in the sessions. This mood may persist for a long time and resist all attempts at interpretation, so that both therapist and patient can feel very 'stuck' in something incomprehensible and unrewarding. The nature of our work being what it is, this mood is often less than comfortable—pointlessness, emptiness, bleakness, a shapeless gloom, an intolerable tension, apathy—I can recall all these words being used by different patients at different times. If one can resist the urge to 'do something', or to escape, or to give up (and the impulse can become as powerful as the mood itself); if one can allow oneself to enter into it and stay with what can feel quite unbearable, only then does some kind of comprehension emerge.

Time and again, what I have found contained within that mood is the wordless experience of how it felt to be a very small child in that particular family, at a time before language and before coherent thought. Once that is understood and put into some kind of words, it can be talked about. The mood miraculously disperses, and the therapy moves on.

Sometimes a different, more transitory mood, is reached. A sense of calm and contentment pervades the therapeutic relationship, a sense of oneness such that time and distance have little meaning. One is reluctant to break the spell. At this point one knows that for this particular patient there was something good at the beginning of life, and in that lies the hope for the future.

(1991)

Personal Perspective

Recently, a friend was telling me of his time spent working on the post-war ill-fated Ground-Nut Scheme. As a young doctor specialising in environmental medicine, he had had great fun, living with his new wife under very primitive conditions far removed from the constraints and frustrations of civilised life. That scheme, for those readers too young to remember, was a brave attempt to use western technology to improve the lot of third-world countries by growing vast quantities of food on hitherto virgin land. Sadly, it failed because the highly skilled and knowledgeable experts had failed to predict the leaching and impoverishment of the soil that rapidly takes place once the surface scrub is removed, and where there is neither the wealth nor the supportive technology necessary to provide artificial fertilisers. It also failed, I was told, because the whole concept of the scheme came not from local demand but from enthusiastic outsiders with little local knowledge and connection. It suffered the fate of so many good ideas and practices (including that of the democratic process itself) exported from a highly developed area of the world to one not yet ready to use them.

I was contrasting this experience with the ideas behind the Intermediate Technology charity whose demands for support come thudding through my letter-box from time to time. This is a charity

35

which is run, I suspect, by a handful of enthusiasts and on a shoe-string budget. It, also, aims to provide technological help to third-world people, but starts from a very different basis. Firstly, the initiative must come from the locals themselves. Then the scheme has to be small, specific and related to day-to-day life, where a small improvement (for example, a deeper well) can make a marked difference to the quality of that life.

Finally, the improvement has to be such that the locals can maintain it for themselves, and learn how to reproduce the skills and technology when needed. In this way, the expertise becomes integrated into the local population, and provides impetus for further change. It seems to work, giving enterprising people what they need at minimum financial outlay, and without creating emotional dependency.

I find myself linking this train of thought with our own area of expertise. When I first began to be interested in matters psychodynamic, the level of insight within the general population was abysmally low. Outside a small circle of people working in London, there were very few sympathetic souls with whom one could begin to share thoughts and feelings on such matters. Over the years, though, counselling has developed as a grass-roots activity, the counselling community has spread its tentacles far and wide, and with it has come the need for a more specialised understanding of unconscious dynamics.

The Samaritans were one of the first organisations in this field (founded, I think, in 1946). Although their brief was always to listen and befriend, rather than counsel, their work brought a need for support and supervision from more highly trained people. The Marriage Guidance Council came into being even earlier, in 1938, initially with a rather practical advice-giving orientation, but post-war saw a change of emphasis and the need for an understanding of such very basic issues as projection and projective identification, splitting, denial and dissociation—a long way from the 'middle-class do-gooders' image! Some clergy, always at the sharp end of human distress in their pastoral work, began to demand help to enable them to cope with stresses which often baffled and sometimes threatened them, in both their inner and outer worlds.

Resource persons were hard to find, and sometimes came from unlikely directions. Psychiatrists could be disappointing, psychiatric social workers a real strength before their specific training disappeared with the creation of the generic social worker; but the powerhouse from which skill and understanding emanated was almost always London—the Institute of Psychoanalysis and the S.A.P. for the theoretical understanding, the Tavistock for the practical application (sometimes routed through other bodies, of course; the Grubb Institute comes to mind.)

With the Sixties came another wave of counselling activities with a strong D.I.Y. element—encounter groups, co-counselling, gestalt, humanistic psychotherapy, bio-energetics, primalling, re-birthing. My feelings about some of the happenings of that era were, and are, ambivalent. Some people were enormously helped, others became casualties. Undeniably a generation was created for whom feelings, emotional insight and personal interaction were a matter of course and normal subjects of conversation.

Now we have arrived at the point when, if there is a national catastrophe such as the sinking of a cross-channel ferry or a football stadium disaster, not just the professionals but the media, the ubiquitous television news, talks of the need for counselling support, and is realistic as to how long it takes to come to terms with such individually momentous events.

I am talking in terms of a ground-swell movement in which I would put analysis (of various schools) at the cutting edge, and psychoanalytical psychotherapy not far behind. However, we need to remember that the many steps forward have each been taken by a single creative individual or small group. For each of them, it was a brave leap into the unknown with only their own intuition to guide them, and minimal support. If now the developments seem inevitable, it required much faith, ingenuity and hard work to bring something substantial into being.

Horses for courses! Creators are one kind of being, sustainers and consolidators another. In the business world, it is commonplace to talk of 'growers' and 'mowers', and generally understood that these are two quite different kinds of personalities, and that both are necessary at different phases of a company's life. I think I would want to add a third type, the 'loner'—the oddball, the eccentric, the unclubbable. Inventors are frequently like this; so are artist-craftsmen. In large organisations they are tolerated to varying degrees because their thought processes are slightly off-beat, and this can be a useful counterfoil to the rest. Their contribution is often not recognised until years later, when they are safely dead and no longer a thorn in anyone's flesh!

In S.I.P. terms, we have had our creative founders, and now we perhaps need a period of consolidation and building on those foundations. I hope, too, that we shall always find room for our quota of 'loners', since many psychotherapists seem naturally to fit that category. If as a profession we can't find a place for the odd-balls, the eccentrics, there is a danger that true creativity will move elsewhere (or worse, that all that potentially fruitful energy will be dissipated in schismatic in-fighting, which would be a poor advertisement for our soi-disant expertise!)

It has been interesting for me to watch the infantile development of the S.I.P. at the same time as my personal retirement beckons. As I write, I am acutely aware that the struggles of one generation have little meaning for the next. What now faces those in the thick of their professional life, and those just entering the work, is the whole question of registration and standardisation of training, and the S.I.P. is indeed fortunate in the doughty political skills of its representatives on the national scene. At the same time, multi-cultural issues impinge ever more closely both from Europe and our own ethnic minorities.

Psychotherapy still has a way to go before it becomes a taken-for-granted part of the social scene in Britain, at least outside London. We are all a part of that on-going process, and it is interesting to compare colleagues' individual professional histories as they move from London to the provinces, welcome incomers on to their own cabbage patch, or move from one place to another in a country riddled with subcultures.

I hope that members will feel able to share their own experiences. I hope, too, that we shall maintain that historical perspective which enables us to value the variety of our members, and particularly that variety of experience which brought the S.I.P. into being.

(1992)

Working-class Therapists

During our collective journey around cultural difference *(SIP Spring Study Day, March, 1992: Individuals & Culture)* a senior member commented on the dearth of working-class people in our profession. His words have remained in my memory as I have struggled with certain patients and certain issues in my consulting-room.

In one sense what he said was certainly, and inevitably, true. By the time someone has traversed the English educational system to the point where he/she can be considered a possible candidate for a psychotherapy training, that person will have entered willy-nilly the professional middle-class. In another sense it is certainly not true. There are, to my personal knowledge, a number of people among our members and trainees who have their roots in working-class culture, and who carry that inheritance within them as part of their life-experience.

Immediately here I am up against the difficulty that arises in attempting to classify people in a way that falsely suggests homogeneity. In reality 'the working class' encompasses an

40

enormous variety of life-styles, attitudes and expectations. Life in an industrial city is very different from life in a village—an obvious example. The television soap-operas *Coronation Street, Eastenders, Brookside* and *Pobol y Cwm* located as they are in different parts of the British Isles, portray very different communities, but their considerable and compulsive popularity suggests that the viewers readily recognise the only slight caricatures which they see on their screens.

Some apparently working-class families are actually submerged middle-class, where there is some knowledge, if sometimes half-forgotten, of a different kind of life-style; and, frequently, hope invested in the children of achieving it again.

Those whose origins are in the Celtic fringe cannot properly be classified in this way since the Celts do not have a class system as such but a clan one. That is not to say that there is no pecking order, but its ramifications are quite different; and submerged or crypto Celts tend to conduct themselves in a way that ignores class distinctions, for good or ill.

These are just a few of the many subtle shades of differentiation that can be found within the English class system. Those who were reared within that system find these matters of compelling interest; others, I imagine, can find them ineffably boring.

I raise them in this forum because I believe they have relevance to our professional concerns. They have relevance in particular to those involved with training. I believe that we have people in our midst who are not accurately perceived, and who consequently are not sufficiently valued in their achievements and struggles, or properly understood in their difficulties.

I believe, too, that it has relevance to our client population. However intuitive we are as therapists, there are limits to our understanding unless there is enough shared experience between therapist and patient. We raised these kinds of issues when we considered work with ethnic minorities. I would suggest that the gaps in cultural understanding that we talked of then are little greater than those that can be experienced between people from very different class backgrounds within our supposedly single culture. If we are to extend psychotherapy more successfully to people of working-class backgrounds, we need more therapists who come out of that background.

Why are there relatively so few of them? The answer lies, I believe, in the traditional English working-class attitude to education, which is all too often one of disinterest and suspicion. (I emphasise English here, because the Celts, however impoverished, have always valued the poet and the scholar.)

It is interesting to ask where this negative attitude comes from. My fantasy is that it goes back to the Norman conquest when William brought over his own clergy as part of his imposed power structure. They acted not only as the civil service but also as the secret police; and the indigenous populace knew it. Since the Church was the guardian of learning and literacy in those days, the conquered, in protecting themselves from being spied upon and bullied, also cut themselves off from the sources of intellectual development. Instead was substituted a dogged collectivism and pressure to conform to the group mores at all costs, traces of which we see still in the trade union movement.

A person from that kind of background needs to be exceptionally bright, able and dogged, and preferably have some outside support or mentor, if he/she is to achieve within our educational system. The price paid is all too often to become emotionally cut off from one's family and childhood friends—to be severed from one's roots. The struggle to achieve is matched by the struggle not to be sabotaged from behind.

It is arguable whether the task is harder for women or for men. Women tend to be subjected more to the pressure to conform, and perhaps find it harder to resist the emotional blackmail. However, they can find a kind of solution by marriage. (This is a dubious solution if they then go on to have children, since it is women who carry the family culture in terms of child-rearing, and they need to identify with their own mothers if they are not to feel totally lost and disoriented in that role.)

Men do not have this option. If more freedom and licence to 'behave badly' is traditionally allowed them as they grow towards adulthood, when they attempt to achieve, they do so on their own.

What then are the characteristics of men and women from this kind of background which might help us recognise them? The answer is not easy since a common characteristic is a tendency to hide. When you are moving into strange social territory, the sensible reaction is to lie low until you understand the rules of the game. In particular, you learn both at home and out there how to avoid the ever-threatening mockery directed at those who are 'different.'

However, this is hardly diagnostic since psychotherapists as a group are good at hiding themselves and waiting; it is a part of our professional armoury, and cultivated as such.

In addition, I have noticed a certain quality of separateness in such people. It can be experienced in a variety of ways—as a sturdy independence of mind and refusal to bow to group pressures; as being unclubbable; as being awkward and difficult; as bloody-minded obstinacy; as a certain isolation; as 'not quite one of us'. The face does not fit!

It can be accompanied by an attitude of mind encapsulated in the phrase, 'won't be told'! This can be maddening to those trying to be helpful, but makes sense once one understands that what was 'told' by those in authority to the young person was all too often inappropriate, irrelevant or misleading, and at odds with that person's growing awareness. (These attitudes can, of course, develop for quite other reasons, such as madness in the family, and again are not diagnostic in themselves!)

There are other give-aways. They can be late developers. There is often a gap between obvious potential and actual achievement, as if the person concerned cannot quite 'make it' to success. If you do not have a parent who can function well out there in the world, showing you how to do and how to be, learning those skills for oneself can be slow, difficult and painful, and the probability is that one never feels as totally comfortable with them as if they had always been a part of one's social repertoire. It is difficult not to envy those who seem to have such skills without even knowing that they have them.

Thus there is a often a discrepancy between intellectual skills and social skills. Not uncommonly there is a similar gap between verbal and literary fluency, an observation made to me many years ago by a psychiatrist of some percipience and wisdom. He pointed out that talking is learned at home, but writing at school—two different skills learned from different teachers with differing levels of achievement.

Also, influencing the perceived social facade, there can be a hidden burn-out factor. The struggle takes its toll. As a professional man of working-class origin commented, you feel exhausted by the time you get to the starting-post!

What you might ask, has all this to do with psychotherapy? This is outer-world stuff, impressionistic and speculative at that. True; but I think it is interesting to us within SIP on two counts. One is that I think we have here a learning opportunity which we are not adequately utilising, which, if explored, would enable us to better facilitate the development of certain individuals within our ambit. In addition, such an exploration could add perspective and depth to some of our clinical work.

We are talking about the experience of certain individuals and a certain group which historically has suffered more than most a high level of narcissistic injury. (This argument also applies to certain ethnic groups, in our society, notably the Afro-Caribbean.) Narcissistic injury leads to narcissistic rage and this is ignored at our peril as Kohut has pointed out, (and as we see all too close to home in the troubles of Northern Ireland.)

Also, somewhere in the middle of all this is the figure of the internalised parent, and what happens when that figure is experienced as absent or inadequate or debased. In one sense it is a problem we all have to face as we become aware that our parent-figures (real or internal) are no longer adequate sources of wisdom and strength as we move into a world that is not theirs and which they do not understand. It is perhaps only at this point that we become truly adult.

The scenario I have described is one where that realisation comes too early, before the individual has the maturity to cope. As so often in our work, timing is all. It is only when the stressing is too soon and too great that we can talk of deprivation and pathology.

(1993)

A Two-edged Experience

I recently spent a few days in a city I knew intimately in my youth. It is not, I must add, a place that I much like or feel identified with, but it contains many memories for me. It has, of course, changed since I lived there. A once respectable working-class district is now the red-light area complete with drug trafficking, while an erstwhile Dickensian slum has been replaced with a pleasant and imaginative new estate, though without the corner shops, ramshackle work sheds and through traffic which kept the old place humming. The one-way road system is horrendous and has involved the sacrifice of one of the oldest and most interesting bits of town. On the other hand, the cultural life, always good, has developed and expanded and is now very lively indeed.

Of my brief visit, two incidents stand out. One was a quick tour around the local industrial museum. This was found by chance, tucked away amongst the domestic offices of a local great house, itself visited only to fill an unscheduled hour. Old cars and beam engines do not normally excite me, but as I dawdled in the wake of my enthusiastic companion I unexpectedly found myself re-drawing the map of my childhood landscape. Here were names

46

that I knew, but had never associated with this locality; names of old cars and motor-bikes that evoke hushed reverence amongst the aficionados. Here were the machines that filled the factories that I used to pass regularly during my routine life in this place. That very familiar road, whose odd name often caused me to speculate, had housed a small workshop producing a very early, unique type of car. That village, which to me meant an open-air swimming pool and summer expeditions with bicycling friends, was the home of a man who had made a knitting machine for stockings back in Tudor times! So many of the city's artefacts, those taken-for-granted bits of the urban landscape, had been designed and built in the last century by young men in their twenties, already holding positions of considerable authority at an age when their descendants of today would still be grubbing away at their Ph.D.s.

I had a sense of the creativity of this place, the skills and imagination, the ingenuity and drive which made the industrial revolution; a different kind of history than anything I was taught at school, but which nonetheless underpins the life we live today—however we may feel about that!

The second incident was when I learned of the existence locally of a coterie of people engaging in perverse sexual practices, and of the involvement of someone known personally to me. I was saddened but not surprised.

I recalled how, many years ago, I was attempting to work with a couple in marital therapy. In spite of my best efforts, we got nowhere and I experienced considerable frustration. It was only during my final meeting with the wife that she admitted what she had hitherto strenuously denied, namely, that her relationship with her close woman friend was an actively sexual one. At this point, everything fell into place. The case made sense and I ceased to feel inadequate and guilty at the lack of progress, since she made it clear that she had never had any intention of repairing the marriage, but had been simply going through the motions, hoping to keep her secret intact.

The news of the sado-masochistic coterie had a similar effect upon me, like adding the final piece to a jigsaw puzzle. All sorts of things that did not quite make sense were clarified, loose ends were tied in, apparently unrelated incidents, disquieting feelings, became part of the total pattern. There was a sense of relief.

I was not surprised because, somehow, it is in the ambience of the place. Nor am I the only one to feel it. I recently watched a short television series—a detective drama *(Resnick. BBC 2)*—set in this city, viewing it for the locations. I recognised only a few of these, but what I did recognise was the feel of the place. With uncanny accuracy, the film-makers and actors had captured it—the depressing, ugly unkemptness of the environment; the hard, aggressive edge in interpersonal relationships; the characteristic style and dress of the women; the tawdry glamour, the dearth of tenderness and loyalty in often exploitive sexual relationships that at times breach acceptable boundaries; the rumbling violence that could explode murderously; the absence of the humour that can relieve a Liverpool. I knew the place was that bad in my inner world. It was confirming to realise it was not just my own projection.

Two sides of a city, two aspects of a culture, with somewhere a link between. I am not suggesting naively that individual psychopathology is the result of social conditioning. Sexual perversion, I would guess, occurs in all cultures and at all social levels within a single culture. The Marquis de Sade and von Sacher-Masoch were both aristocrats. However, when a certain kind of behaviour exhibits a social dimension, then I think we are entitled to ask if there is something in that society which encourages the behaviour, or at least tacitly gives it permission.

The agrarian revolution which drove people off the land and into the towns, the industrial revolution which exploited their too-cheap labour, degraded the lives of the working-classes in the eighteenth and nineteenth centuries. It destroyed the rural communities, cut off their cultural roots, and gave them little in exchange beyond a bare subsistence living. It can be argued that their housing standards were no worse—rural poverty could be grim, too—but their environment was degraded, their working conditions were debased, and their health with it. How much so

48

only surfaced with the advent of compulsory military service during the 1914-18 war, when a high proportion of men were rejected as unfit.

I do not see how people can live in the kind of conditions that were the norm in the slums of the industrial revolution without it reflecting back into all areas of their inner life, including the sexual one. Where privacy is hard to find; where walls are thin; where children share beds with adults; where siblings of both sexes share bedrooms into adolescence and beyond, it becomes hard to maintain appropriate boundaries, or a proper sense of self-respect. Where men feel belittled by the work they do, where women feel undermined by the interminable and ineffectual battle against grime, it is hard for them to be tender and loving towards each other and their children. Where there are too many people in too small an area, limits and boundaries crumble under the strain; the management of aggression takes a lot of psychic energy and depression is a common outcome.

If these conditions seems to belong to the nineteenth century rather than this one, I can personally vouchsafe that they still existed thirty to forty years ago, which means that we meet people in the patient population who grew up in these circumstances. I am not suggesting that psychopathology is the inevitable result, but I am suggesting that one cannot ignore the impact of that outer world upon the inner.

I think of my patient Q. who came from this kind of background. He has reacted by developing an obsessional persona, fanatically clean and neat in his person, and determined to live in a material style to match. Much of his wealth and energy goes into making the perfect home. In his job he is a workaholic, extremely organised and demanding much of his subordinates. Within this framework, surprisingly, he can allow himself to be highly creative. He has talents which would have probably have brought him an artistic education, given a different background. As it is, he has found an industrial niche where he can use them in a much-valued way, in the tradition of his forebears, and he has a number of artistic hobbies which he enjoys. He is fortunate in his wife who has a

49

similar background, and they form a mutually supportive, not to say collusive, system.

I suspect that his obsessional defences protect him from a latent psychosis. (His mother sounds psychotically depressed in a chronic, low-grade way.) He came to see me after lengthy and unsuccessful investigations for a curious variety of physical symptoms which were never adequately explained. They seemed to me to be a manifestation of an anxiety-depression following the death of his father from cancer, and an aspect of his bereavement reaction. He has remarkable little insight for such an intelligent man, and finds it hard to believe that his (to him) odd feelings can have any meaning. However, his symptoms have retreated, and although he doesn't really believe the 'explanations' I offer, he knows that talking to me makes him feel better. I sense that the underlying threat is of impending disintegration and chaos. Although I have abandoned the hope of luring him into therapy proper, he comes to see me whenever his anxiety levels become unmanageably high. This is characteristically when he feels his working situation is not properly under his control, when there is a change or threatened change in the authority structure, when there is just too much to possibly accomplish. I suspect, and I think he knows, that to come into therapy would face him with a massive depression which would interfere with his work and his creativity, and neither of us wants to deal with that. (If we have to at some future date, that is another matter.) I used to feel sad for him that he and his wife never felt the need for children. Now I think it was probably a wise decision. The resultant situation might have been too much for him to adapt to.

X. is another fish from the same kettle, but of a more robust temperament. He acquired street wisdom at an early age, and went through a phase of near-criminal delinquency in his adolescence. As a young man, he entered into a sexual relationship that was perversely inappropriate in a social sense, with a woman whose various liaisons had a strongly sado-masochistic flavour. At this point, when real disaster loomed, he took his life in hand and found himself a girl-friend who was very straight and direct, and who had the ego-strength to manage him and do battle when necessary. He has since become a respectable and successful member of the bourgeoisie. He has found in his work an outlet for all the energy and creativity that he exhibited in his youth, and he operates in a sub-culture where a certain mild delinquency is tolerated and can indeed bring rewards as long as it is kept within bounds. He has never broken down and is unlikely, I would judge, ever to do so, since at times of crisis he has always managed to muster ego-strength and transform his situation.

His apparent success is built, of course, on a degree of splitting. If I do not worry for him, I do have some concern for the next generation, since this man, unlike Q., has felt able to have a family, and indeed works hard to give them the quality of life he would have liked for himself. I cannot but wonder how much of what is now denied is lying dormant in the unconscious of this family, and whether it will re-emerge in some form of acting-out by the young.

I note that both these men have moved far away from the environment in which they were reared, but that they each have siblings who returned, and whose lives are currently disordered, and destructive to those around them.

I am searching, I realise, for the links between the shared outer world and the private inner worlds of those few people I feel I know well enough to comment upon. The vicissitudes of human development are difficult enough at the best of times. When they take place against a background where it is almost impossible to provide good-enough parenting; where the parental models are all too often denigrated figures; where the fabric of the environment is literally crumbling into dirt and decay; it is hardly surprising if the inner world sometimes reflects back that disintegration of structure and difference that is the pervert's anal inner world.

Back to the sado-masochistic sexual coterie that sparked this line of thought. What saddens me is that I am sure that it embodies within it some kind of hope; some attempt to integrate experiences that contain pain, loneliness and bewilderment; some excitement to keep at bay a level of depression and alienation that threatens to make life meaningless; some sensory stimulation that confirms embodiment and protects from the danger of falling into the abyss.

Sharing eases the tensions. I would like to think that for some of its members, it may prove to be a growth experience. My limited understanding of this complex and difficult area of human experience makes me both doubtful and fearful.

(1993)

Post-script

Since writing this piece, the individual who was my primary concern appears to have emerged from what, in retrospect, was a transitory phase. I think the experience may be understood as an idiosyncratic reaction to two concurrent bereavements in someone who was too brittle to mourn properly.

In the meantime, more than one patient has spontaneously complained to me about the quantity and quality of sado-masochistic material impinging upon them from the various media; and the recent appalling deaths of James Bulger, Suzanne Capper and the five victims of Colin Ireland* have disquieted us all.

While the particular factor alluded to in this piece was undoubtedly significant for the individuals concerned, there are many other boundary issues at work in our wider society today. Many of them are linked, I suspect, to the considerable geographical and social mobility we have experienced within British society during the latter half of this century. The Sixties, too, were a time when boundaries were dissolving in all directions. In retrospect, the period has a slightly manic feel about it comparable to the 'flapper' era of the Twenties. That phenomenon was an undoubted reaction to the horrors of the 1914-18 war. The Sixties revolution was brought about by children growing up in the still bleak and dreary Forties and Fifties, amongst the shattered structures (both material and social) of the post-war years, with parents who were only too willing to forget the harsh discipline the war had imposed on everyone, and who were happy to indulge their young in the hope of better things to come.

The increased availability of contraception, particularly the advent of the Pill, fuelled the rapid change in sexual mores and behaviour begun during the 1939-45 period. The traditional modes of containment became inadequate with consequences both good and ill.

While these factors are not primary in terms of our professional focus, the intra-psychic development of the individual, I cannot but feel that they have tended to facilitate a sense of disorientation, and regression to that perverse anal-sadistic world so powerfully described by Chasseguet-Smirgel, rather than to support the always difficult struggle towards increasing differentiation and integration which is the ongoing task of growth and maturation.

* *James Bulger was a two-year old child who was abducted while out shopping with his mother by two slighly older boys, and subsequently killed by them. Suzanne Capper was a sixteeen-year old girl who was systematically and horribly tortured for eight days before being murdered by her captor. Colin Ireland was a serial killer of homosexual men.*

(1994)

Anniversaries

Anniversaries have a symbolic significance way beyond the actuality—witness the recent difficulties surrounding the Fiftieth VE-Day celebrations.* I have known otherwise sane and sensible men and women grow near-hysterical at the approach of their Thirtieth or Fortieth birthday, while the 'Big 60' clearly has awesome implications for some.

Anniversary celebrations have a knack of revealing a usually hidden level of truth in the psychodynamics of those concerned, whether the individual or the group. A recent family golden wedding ran into logistic problems. In retrospect, I can reflect with a certain wry amusement on how characteristic were the responses of those involved, and how the very difficulties reflected the nursery dynamics of forty years ago.

Perhaps some of the point of such celebrations is that they give us the opportunity to re-visit the past, to evaluate it and, hopefully, to move on—to make internal adjustments which may lay some ghosts, resolve outstanding difficulties, reconcile us to what cannot be changed.

I sometimes think it a pity that while we are punctilious in our society about celebrating some things, others pass unnoticed. For example, death-days. I have had patients who routinely get

54

depressed at a certain time each year for no apparent reason that they can acknowledge. It often needs only a little work for them to 'remember' that that particular time of the year was the time of a significant bereavement. What is surprising is that they have such difficulty every year in 'remembering'—in holding on to the knowledge that they have. Perhaps some pain never does become totally manageable, however much 'working-through' we do.

A woman parked her car outside her home which was situated on a hill. She had been unduly low for a couple of weeks for no apparent reason. That day she forgot to put the handbrake on. When she came out to find the car again, she couldn't believe her eyes. It had rolled in an arc into the wall on the opposite side of the road, and was more than a little crumpled. A momentary inattention had caused extensive, and expensive, damage. It was only at that point that she recalled that it was, to the day, the anniversary of the death of one of her children, and that the current incident mirrored that original event when a moment of inattention had led to such dire results.

This year marks the Tenth anniversary of the founding of SIP—a short time in the life of an established institution, but significant for a young one like ours. Those who nurtured it at the beginning, those who have watched it grow in size and complexity, those who have changed status within it, will feel the import of those years.

It has been a time of enormous change, not only for SIP but for the profession as a whole. I have heard many complaints recently from the students of a training body in a related field of how the institution has kept changing the goal-posts during their training. These complaints have been particularly vociferous from those whose training has been inadvertently lengthy. They find it difficult to hear what I keep saying to them—namely, that the goal-posts have indeed kept changing for the profession as a whole, that we all find it stressful, and that it isn't 'fair'. (I am actually very sympathetic—such changes can feel like the last straw on an intolerably burdensome journey.)

It is a tribute to those who have carried the major burden of managing SIP during these crucial formative years that we have negotiated the difficulties so well. They have had to manage not only the problems which we increasingly understand as a normal part of organisational growth and development, but they have had to do it against a backdrop of rapidly changing standards and expectations from outside, the political shenanigans which always accompany such change, and all this in a wider society which grows ever more litigious.

We must be grateful for the creative vision which brought SIP into being, and for the wisdom, skill and commitment (and sheer hard slog!) which has brought it to its current position.

We have cause to celebrate.

(1995)

* There was a great deal of controversial discussion in the press prior to the fiftieth anniversary of VE-Day as to the manner in which the nation should celebrate, or whether it was even appropriate to do so. Feelings ran high for some.

Racism

- *At the time this piece was written racism was becoming an emotive issue, particularly for people living and working in areas of mixed ethnic communities. The following reaction was sparked by a document sent to us from a working group under the auspices of our professional umbrella body, UKCP. It suggested that all 'white' people were unconsciously and deeply racist, and that our professional practice needed to be modified in acknowledgment of that ineradicable factor. I found the arguments unconvincing.*

I must confess to an automatic 'reaching for my gun' at the use of the term 'black' to describe people whose skin colour ranges from a deep chocolate brown to a pale coffee with various shades of olive in between. I also fail to see what is culturally in common, except humanity, between Afro-Caribbeans, Arabs, Asians of different groups and religions, Australian aborigines and the multiplicity of African peoples, all of whom I have seen included under the umbrella term of 'black'.

My earliest exposure to racial difference was as a medical student. My year cohort included a girl from Trinidad with a very dark skin, and a somewhat paler Christian Arab from Palestine. They were as different from each other as from the rest of the group, but within weeks had been absorbed as just two more fellow students, as indeed were the small handful of men and the equally small handful of mature students amongst us. If they had some difficulty in adjusting to metropolitan life, they seemed more at ease than those few students from non-professional family backgrounds, or the small group from rural Wales.

Subsequently, living as a staff member in a university hall of residence also brought some interesting experiences. The young 'black' African who had never ever slept on his own, and was deeply disturbed at being isolated in a single room; the strange grimaces and gestures of another young man from that continent which looked quite crazy until we learned the meaning of his non-verbal communications. Neither was any more disadvantaged than the student from a very working-class Midland background who was so acutely miserable that he wet his bed every night for a week and finally fled never to return. Equally disadvantaged was the young man whose first language was Welsh, and who was a considerable poet in that language. Sadly, his grasp of English was so poor that his engineering examination marks were well below expectations. His discouragement and depression were so deep that he withdrew after a long struggle. It seemed a terrible waste.

If we are talking about groups of people being downtrodden, the most downtrodden people I ever met were some groups of Russian teachers sent to this country to improve their English. They were chronically and distressingly terrified (apart from their 'minders' who were relaxed, expansive and charming!)

I suppose I am saying that for me personally and professionally, I have never been able to escape from the subtleties of cultural difference, and I don't need it thrust down my throat. That seems to me to be the reality for my fellow psychotherapists, too, as far as I can tell.

If the complaint is that the Anglo-Saxons are not very warm and welcoming to minority groups, I don't think they ever have been. (On the other hand they have accepted, tolerated and finally integrated very many people who have sought a haven on their shores.) The history of the Celtic peoples in the British Isles is full of examples of barbarous and insensitive behaviour by the powers-that-be towards them, some of them such as the Welsh 'not', not so very distant in time. The Jews experienced widespread anti-Semitism here in the Thirties; the Irish were similarly held in contempt. Working-class people have often felt despised by the rest, 'the establishment' threatened by 'declining standards'.

We can all find good reasons 'out there' for the paranoia which we carry inside us. As psychotherapists, surely our primary duty is not to collude with these phantasies, which is what I feel this document is asking us to do.

Having said that, am I missing something? Is it perhaps that the experience of slavery in one's relatively recent cultural past leaves a profound narcissistic wound? Where there has been real scapegoating, is this what then evokes the projections? There seems to be room for a discussion about scapegoating as practised by groups. As an individual phenomenon, we have some understanding of it since we meet it often enough in our work, but I suspect there is a body of literature on group phenomena that I would like to know more about.

Finally, for me, there is the whole question of a multi-cultural society. Can it really be made to work? Recent history is not encouraging. The devastation of the once highly-civilised Lebanon, the fate of the Kurds in Iraq, are too recent for comfort. The problem for our members living in the West Country is rarely pressing, but those still working, or recently working, in London will have a different perspective.

Perhaps social pain and social neurosis need to be met in the same way as the individual variety—by careful listening, by acknowledgment of the pain, acknowledgment of the reality of deprivation and what that does to the human psyche, by acknowledgment of the failure on the part of those who should have known better or cared more. Would the Irish problem still be with us if the history of Ireland was as well known to the English as their own? However, as we know all too well from our consulting room practice, there is still a world of difference between 'understanding' and 'feeling with', and submitting to emotional blackmail!

Let us not forget, too, that there is such a thing as social psychosis, and how do we respond to that?

(1996)

The Welsh 'not' was a piece of wood bearing the inscription 'Not' hung about the neck of schoolchildren heard speaking Welsh. It was part of a deliberate attempt by the powers-that-be to replace the Welsh language with English. My grandmother could remember its use. She also recalled being beaten for speaking Welsh!

Old Times and New

One of the dominant passions of my life has been books. This has not always met with unqualified approval from the household gods. The protesting voices range from the anything-but-resigned one of, 'That child has always got her nose in a book!' to the more recent, totally resigned one of, 'And where do you think I am going to find a bit of wall solid enough to take yet another bookcase!' Though normally amenable enough, I have resisted these complaints, the first on the grounds of self-defence, the second on the basis of pot-calling-kettle-black. The truth is that the gut-churning excitement that first gripped me the day I enrolled at the local public library has never quite left me.

It was therefore with something of a sense of shock that, on stacking my latest purchase on the shelves, I felt not the usual smug sense of ownership and anticipated delight but something akin to dismay and a sinking of the spirits.

I had finally succumbed to an offer from the British Psycho-Analytical Book Club and bought myself a complete edition of Freud. Well, it was past time! My own collection was always incomplete, a motley group of hard and paperback, and all of it ante-dating the *Standard Edition*. What I had not bargained for was the rush of memories that came flooding back as I stacked these discarded volumes on the floor. Truth was, they embodied aspects of my personal history that I had largely forgotten. That early Pelican of *The Psychopathology of Everyday Life* was my first contact with Freud's writing, and the contents of that and the accompanying volume of *Totem and Taboo* were amongst the first subjects of conversation between myself and my future husband, (and very daring we felt ourselves to be at the mature age of 16!) The treasured five volumes of *Case Histories* were a birthday present and new; most of the rest were unearthed from the dusty recesses of various second-hand bookshops which were my regular adolescent haunts. My first copy of *The Interpretation of Dreams* was 'borrowed' by a student friend, and could only be replaced much later when funds allowed. A panorama of forgotten places and faces were suddenly there again with a Proustian clarity.

Above all, what came flooding back was the sense of excitement, of discovery, the hope and expectation that somewhere in all these volumes lay the key to understanding so much that was puzzling, so many tangles that needed unravelling; and a sort of queer comfort. I realised that those books (and a few others alongside) had acquired something of the characteristics of transitional objects —something to be clung to when the going got rough. Throwing them out now felt a bit like throwing out one's favourite Teddy Bear, and I was gripped by a real sense of bereavement.

Much of the excitement of that voyage of discovery was because it was a very personal exploration. I would not have attempted to share the ideas with the adults of my childhood years—their expected disapproval only added to my commitment. However, it was a bitter blow to find the same rejection from the teachers of my medical student days. I felt, and still feel, they should have known better; but then, it is easy to under-estimate the anxieties attendant upon professional practice in the public eye—anxieties we are just beginning to face as the psychotherapy profession moves towards registration.

What I wonder now, as we move into a different phase, is whether it is still possible for students to encounter Freud with that level and quality of excitement that was my own experience, now that psycho-analytic ideas are so much more widespread and acceptable. In particular, is it possible to feel that way about ideas that are presented as part of a formal training course i.e. promoted and sanctioned by parental figures. In fact, as I write, I can think of one or two students I have taught recently who obviously share that same kind of excitement, but they are mature people who again discovered these ideas for themselves, and only moved into professional training later.

I recently found an echoing passage in Bruno Bettelheim's *Recollections and Reflections*. In the chapter entitled 'How I learned about psychoanalysis' he contrasts the way things are now done in America with the way they were done in the Vienna of his youth.

> 'My interest had been anything but theoretical—from the beginning it had been personal and very emotional, characterised by a belief that psychoanalysis could make a most important difference in one's life; and so it did in mine.

> As far as I know, the pioneers of psychoanalysis came to it in quite different but more or less equally personal and emotionally conditioned ways, and psychoanalysis flourished under their influence.'

> '....It was all a matter of very personal experience. Today an elaborate course of study is required of people wishing to become psychoanalysts and much of the highly personal excitement psychoanalysis created is gone; it has become an institutionalised discipline.'

In another essay, 'Two views of Freud' he says, '...the new movement shared the fate of so many others which began with great courage and high resolve. The original enthusiasm, freshness and spontaneity weakened, and a hierarchy took over which claimed its prestige from the correct interpretation of the dogma and exercised the power to judge who could be counted among the faithful. Eventually dogma, ritual and idolatry toward the leader replaced that leader's creative daring and imagination.'

It is not difficult to detect in Bettelheim's words the nostalgia of an old man for his own youth with its enthusiasm, freshness and spontaneity. Perhaps some of the changes he was commenting on are inevitable as we move from a pioneering discipline to an established one, though I hope that we are not so far along that road in the UK. Perhaps the very lack of acceptance by the medical establishment that I felt so keenly as a student has been a saving grace; and we are a less conformist culture than that of the USA.

Having said all that, it surely behoves those of us who are involved in the training and formation of the next generation of psychotherapists to think hard about what it is we need to pass on —not just the discipline, but the spirit of our founding parents.

(1996)

Shame

There seems to be relatively little psychoanalytical writing on the subject of *shame* as compared to that on *guilt*, so I was interested to come across a paper by Sylvia Amati Mas entitled 'Ambiguity as the route to shame'.

Much of the paper is about the therapy of a woman who had been subjected to stressing of the most extreme kind, to torture and humiliation, and who shortly after her release suffered a miscarriage as the result of her ill-treatment. Understandably, it took considerable patience and time before the woman could begin to use the therapy in such a way as to think about what had happened to her. When she gradually began to talk about her sense of shame at having been treated in such a way, Mas understood this as a signal that she was beginning to recover—in particular, that she was beginning to recover her sense of her own identity and self-worth, and her 'capacity for conflict in regard to the alienation sustained.'

Mas addresses the predicament of those who are subjected to such extreme experiences 'inflicted on them with the explicit intention of disturbing the personality', and who have no option but to endure in the attempt to survive. She believes that under such circumstances, the individual regresses to that state which she calls ambiguity, based on a model put forward by Bleger, which she understands as that very early state of mind, pre-dating Klein's paranoid-schizoid position, when subject and object are still part of a whole—what I would tend to refer to as the symbiotic phase of early development, or primary non-differentiation. Implicit in this regression is the loss of one's sense of who one is, a blurring of the boundaries between self and not-self, a loss of the critical capacity and ability to fight back, and with it all a kind of collusion in what is happening.

Mas believes that the emergence of a sense of shame is related to the regaining of the sense of identity. With it comes anger at how one has been treated, but also shame that one was forced to accept what was done to one, and at the unwilling collusion in an unacceptable scenario as a last-ditch attempt to survive.

Fortunately, few of us in our society are subject to such an extreme experience, though those therapists who have worked with survivors of the Holocaust will no doubt recognise the similarities. I found my mind making connections to other, less appalling, situations which contained some of the same elements. We know, for example, that people who are the victims of kidnapping and who are held for long periods of time, can come to understand and even sympathise with their captors. Occasionally there even develops a sexual relationship with the captor and an identification with his cause—I am thinking here of the Patti Hearst case in the USA.

We know that the victims of sexual abuse characteristically have difficulty in talking about their experience in the way that Mas's patient had. When those victims are children and the abuser is a family member or close family friend, there is frequently a long-term collusion because the victim feels unable to protest or defend, or even to see the behaviour as abusive. We know, too of the powerful sense of shame that these victims subsequently experience.

I find myself, too, thinking of other scenarios, less malignant, more commonplace, which have something of these elements about them.

I recall an elderly man telling me about his sense of shame at having to wear ill-fitting clumsy boots as a child at a time when his family was very poor, and of his ever-lasting gratitude to the kindly neighbour who gave them a polish to encourage him to feel better about himself

I remember, too, as a child, a profound sense of shame at being made to wear clothes which felt just wrong to me and how I wanted to look. (They were perfectly good clothes by adult standards but 'different' from those my peers were wearing and evoked the kind of cruel teasing that children indulge in.) I think too of the battles that are commonplace between adolescents and their parents, when the parents try to impose behaviour that seems reasonable by their adult standards but which the adolescent feels to be a betrayal of his emerging self. The strength of the feelings aroused is indicative that this is more than just a battle of wills, and if the young person has to capitulate he can behave as if deeply ashamed (as well as resentful) at his enforced collusion.

We can probably all think of times when we feel obliged, for social reasons, to be polite to people we thoroughly dislike (perhaps a boss or neighbour we cannot afford to offend) and, too, the situation where we find ourselves provoked by others' unreasonable behaviour into thinking thoughts or behaving in a way we do not like or wish to own. Our ego-ideal is breached, and we can feel ashamed at allowing ourselves to be stressed to such a degree.

I have become aware of the sense of shame experienced by the children of highly narcissistic parents. Since such parents have little sense of the 'other', they have little capacity to act as mirror to their children. In order to gain any attention, and the emotional supplies a child needs from its parents, it is obliged to pretend it is something it is not—it has to collude with the parents' fantasy of who their child is, and deny or suppress who it actually is. The end-result is a poor sense of identity and a vague sense of shame about one's self.

I have found a similar but more extreme scenario among some families of schizophrenics. In these cases, there is not only a failure of mirroring, but also an active denial of the child's experience. When the attempt to achieve some a sense of personal identity finally breaks down, the shame of failure in one's life-task is compounded by scapegoating by the family. (I am not suggesting that this scenario is the sole factor underlying schizophrenia. However, it does seem to be a recognisable pattern in the history of some patients. Whatever one's critical evaluation of the work of R.D.Laing, his book with Aaron Esterson on the families of schizophrenics contains some powerful and moving case-histories illustrating this theme.)

What these different scenarios seem to have in common is a spectrum of betrayal—at the least damaging end, a betrayal of one's ego-ideal, then a betrayal of one's sense of identity from the most superficial understanding of that term to the most profound. If we think of the process of maturation as a process of becoming who we are—in Jungian terms, individuation—then the enforced regression as described by Mas is a profound betrayal of one's deepest self, of one's innate life-task, and ultimately of psychic life itself

It is an awareness of that betrayal that seems to underlie the sense of shame.

(1998)

The Blind Men and the Elephant

I have long been intrigued as to why different people interpret similar experience in such very different ways. Why are we drawn towards one school of thought rather than another? What is it that makes one person a Freudian, another a Jungian, a third Kleinian, a fourth Lacanian etc.?

Undoubtedly there is an element of randomness in those circumstances which make us what we are. One can talk about chance or coincidence, one can invoke Jung's concept of synchronicity, one can point to the exciting ideas embodied in the new theories of chaos, particularly perhaps the notion that very small happenings can have large and unpredictable consequences. You will all have experienced the kind of thing I have in mind; finding the right book at the right time, encountering a seminal idea at just the moment when it speaks to one's condition, the chance meeting with a significant person at a crucial time in one's life when one is searching for a new direction and needing a model or a guru.

Adolescence is perhaps the time par excellence when we can see these factors at work, but I do not think they belong exclusively to that time.

Then there is the influence of our profession of origin—the discipline from which we moved into psychotherapy. Whilst I early rejected the medical model of mental illness, I am aware that my medical studies left me with certain attitudes and orientation which form a largely unverbalised and unconscious backdrop to my thinking and behaviour.

I have a strong sense of what I think of as the biological 'given'—an awareness of Man as a member of the animal kingdom with all that that implies in terms of our phylogenetic history and inheritance. I acquired, with reluctance, a profound respect for those innate needs and drives which we ignore at our peril. I came to appreciate the power of those inbuilt patterns of development, which unfold with their own momentum, and which need to be met with appropriate responses from the environment if the individual is ever to attain anything near his/her potential. Both Donald Winnicott and Michael Fordham address these issues in their writings.

It was during this period of my life that I came, again reluctantly, being in my youth of a distinctly feminist turn of mind, to an appreciation of gender difference! Above all, I was left with a profound sense of the complex and subtle interaction between mind and body, and an abiding interest in psychosomatic disorders.

Well, that is all part of my personal history, and each one of us will have their own equivalent story to tell of how their professional training and experience left its mark upon them.

However, interesting as these ramblings into one's past may or may not be, they beg the essential question; what is it that leads us to respond to certain stimuli in our environment and not others? Why seize some opportunities and ignore others? Why did we choose that profession out of the range of possibilities open to us? The answer lies surely in our own inner world.

I would suggest that we choose a certain orientation, a particular school of thought because it reflects our own inner world.

I would liken it to the falling in love experience. It can happen instantaneously, as when one sees a stranger across a room and there is an electric flash of recognition; it can happen quickly, as when one talks to someone for half an hour and feels one has known them all one's life; it can happy slowly and imperceptibly, as when the other has been around in the background for some time, and only gradually does the realisation dawn that this person has become someone one cannot manage without.

In a comparable way, we can read an author, we can listen to an exposition of some clinical work, we can take something on board in a routine kind of way, and then become aware of a level of excitement intruding into consciousness. Some kind of resonance has been set into motion. There is suddenly a correspondence between our outer and inner worlds. We are into a new ball-game.

For me, personally, this is as good a starting place as any. After all, it is a truism that we come into this work out of our own needs and tensions, and the desire to come to terms with ourselves. Of course, in time that initial surge becomes overlaid by many other factors and there is, one hopes, secondary gain of many kinds. Nonetheless, it is from our own personal psychodynamics that the energy flows.

When we adopt a theoretical orientation that mirrors our own inner world, it has the advantage that we can more quickly make it our own. We can rapidly grasp the subtleties of our subject, we can use our intuitive understanding to feel our way into the dark corners that might otherwise remain obscure.

Above all, a theoretical framework thus chosen feels real. It has meaning and validity for us. It allows us to meet our patients with a sense of integrity that is as important for them as it is for us. However, comfortable as this sounds, and may very well feel, we cannot leave it there, because, whatever its virtues, it is essentially a narcissistic orientation.

Perhaps at this point I should nail my colours to the mast and confess that I see myself as a Freudian of the Middle or Independent group. In the days when I still had time to read extensively, and long before I had even of heard of such a group, it was the authors of this orientation who spoke to my condition. I was stimulated by what they were trying to say, I could link it with my own experience, and I acquired words and concepts which enabled me to think about what had hitherto only been felt. It was sheer chance, for which I am immensely grateful, that my training analyst happened to be of that persuasion; and it was good management on the part of my tutor who found me a sympathetic supervisor after a somewhat (mutually) frustrating earlier experience.

Since then, much has happened, both personally and professionally, but it is in that group that I still feel most at home.

Having said all that, I have to confess that in thinking about my patients I frequently use Kleinian concepts in order to make sense of what is in front of me in the consulting room; that the concept of transmarginal stressing is central to my understanding of schizoid phenomena, (and that derives from Pavlov's work with dogs and so properly belongs to the behaviourist tradition); whilst, particularly towards the end of a long period of therapy when, in my experience, almost all patients, whether of formal religious persuasion or not, begin to ask the ultimate questions—what is life all about, what is *my* life all about—I find myself talking in words that owe more to Jung than to Freud.

I find this somewhat surprising since I am by temperament of a rather obsessional turn of mind, and inclined to plough one particular furrow unless firmly deflected. I can only plead that what has deflected me is the necessity to make sense of what I meet in the consulting room.

I think what I am saying is that, for me, experience comes first; theory follows as a conceptual framework with which to make sense of the experience. Theory is a model, or a series of models; an approximation to the truth, not the truth itself. Good theory has the pragmatic sanction i.e. if it works, use it. If this makes for a few loose ends, a less than coherent whole, so be it. I think we have to live with this, just as we have to live with the fragmentary and unfinished picture of our patients' lives, holding the loose ends and knitting them into a meaningful picture as they unravel. We are still a long way from a comprehensive and unified theory of psychic development and therapeutic practice, and we must not let our anxieties lead us into a premature fossilisation of thought.

I can now look back with amusement to the patient who first made the Kleinian inner world real to me. Of course, I had read Melanie Klein's writings; or to put it more accurately, I had made a number of attempts to struggle with her ideas. Some of it I could relate to, some felt just wrong, but I could not feel it was part of me in a deep and satisfying kind of way.

This particular patient was superficially a well-educated, middle-class, civilised woman. Her friends saw her, so she informed me acerbically, as a nice person, a good friend, sympathetic and helpful. With me she was quite other. From the very first session, she was manipulative and exploitive, ruthless to a degree which left me speechless. She metaphorically bit, scratched, kicked and shat on everything that was offered her. Even I could hardly fail to recognise that I was dealing with a massive negative transference, which intermittently became psychotic. I went back to my Kleinian texts in a desperate attempt to understand and manage the situation, and there it all was! Now I could really understand what was being talked about. .

If I had followed my initial inclination, had there been anyone else to pass her on to, I would have referred her. If I had done so, I should have spared myself a very difficult three years, and I should have missed an invaluable learning experience. (Yes, she did quite well in the end. She got herself on to a training programme, found herself the Kleinian therapist she needed, and was kind enough to say that it was very similar to her experience with me, from which I gathered that her new therapist was also giving her a difficult time!)

She taught me more about the mechanisms of denial, dissociation, evasion, splitting, projection and projective identification in a few months than I had hitherto learned in as many years. Then, having seen these psychic mechanisms at work in such a gross fashion, I found I was seeing their more subtle manifestations in my other patients, then in my nearest and dearest, and finally in myself. (I am still working on that one!)

I quote this one example of how patients will teach us what we need to know if we can only be open to them. I can think of other similar examples from my practice, and any experienced therapist could add their own comparable stories.

So far I have been sharing with you something of my personal journey. There is, however, a quantum leap that needs to be made from the individual saga to the training scheme which must be appropriate to a variety of people with a wide spread of experience. What are the pros and cons of the two approaches to training—the eclectic approach and the focused approach?

The disadvantage of eclecticism is inherent in the many different theories and perspectives which are part of the syllabus. Students on such a training scheme often go through a phase when they feel both confused and irritated by the wealth and variety of information which they are expected to assimilate. Mental indigestion becomes the norm!

The positive aspect of the eclectic approach only becomes apparent as this is worked through, when, hopefully, the student emerges with some appreciation of the multifarious ways there are of experiencing and conceptualising basic human life, and an understanding that different people's inner worlds are very different.

The success of the eclectic method of training is crucially dependent on the individual student's capacity for integration; of his ability to fuse several perspectives into a coherent whole. This is a tall order, and may well be a lifetime's work!

A focused training of whatever school has some immediately obvious advantages. There will be less confusion, less dissipation of mental energy, more coherence, and the end result is likely to be a student with a higher level of technique because more time and effort has been available to achieving just that.

This in itself is attractive because we all have a high investment in technique. We put a great deal of time and energy into achieving it;

and having achieved it, we experience pleasure in exercising it. It becomes the basis of professional approbation, and we use it as a yardstick with which to measure ourselves against our colleagues. It can be demonstrated and examined and discussed, and that makes us feel we are being 'scientific' and therefore respectable.

However, 1 think we need to ask ourselves, is it technique that makes for therapeutic success? The answer is, of course, yes—in part. We have only to work with a more experienced colleague to realise how much we have missed, how much better we could have handled that particular session. We have only to think back to our first clients to realise how much our skills have developed since that time.

Having said that, such few independent investigations that have been made suggest that therapeutic success has little or no correlation with either the length of training of the therapist or the orientation of that training. What it does seem to correlate with are certain human qualities, some characteristics of temperament and disposition which can be recognised and named, if not readily measured.

I suspect the truth is that, in order to serve our patients as well as they need, we must have both the human qualities and the trained skills. What we must beware of doing is destroying one in our search for the other. It can happen, and I believe has happened in certain not too distant professions.

I must confess to a certain bias in this area. I have known people with minimal training who have done very good work with very disturbed clients. They did it partly because they did not have the experience to know that what they were trying to do was impossible!

What they did have was time and patience, and above all, hope; and with support they were able to keep that hope alive for their patients even when those patients had lost it for themselves. Sometimes, too, they needed support in order to survive their patients' attacks, and to understand the underlying meaning, but I never found that they lacked courage.

What they were not able to do was describe their work in a step-by-step analytical way which would communicate the process to others, and which others could learn from. They were not able to put their work into a well-conceptualised theoretical framework which they could then use to illuminate theoretical points, and perhaps to expand and extend existing theory. In other words, they could not put forward their work as a piece of research material, which all good analytical work is.

However, do we all need to be research workers? It is undeniable that in any subject, research is the life-blood, and without it that subject becomes stale and deteriorates.

However, it is generally accepted both in the academic world and in industry that research workers are a breed unto themselves. They have of necessity highly focused minds; they tend to be passionate about their own subject and disinterested in much outside it. They need sensitive and firm management since they tend to be ruthless in pursuit of their own ends, particularly in appropriating any available funds, and if allowed a free rein will distort the group life of their firm or institution. This admirable single-mindedness of purpose derives from the high level of satisfaction that the work brings, (and the hoped-for kudos when it is successful!) However, there does need to be someone who is sufficiently detached to keep asking the all-important questions—who, or what, is it for? What is the price to be paid, and who is paying it?

There is a strong argument for giving students the best possible technical training on the grounds that once out in the field, standards will inevitably fall. This is true if, once qualified, people are on their own. It is surely less relevant in the context of the psychotherapeutic tradition, where it is taken for granted that practitioners will seek further supervision and therapy as and when needed. One could indeed argue that this practice is so well entrenched that it has militated against the spread of psychoanalytical psychotherapy outside the metropolis until very recently!

Surely, at the end of the day, we want to produce therapists who are still enthusiastic, eager to learn, and open to the possibility of further exploration.

I feel that the greatest danger of a focused training is that of falling into the arrogance of believing that our kind of inner world is all there is, that we and our colleagues have all the answers. We all know of Freudians who seem unaware of life beyond the Oedipus complex; of Jungians who are so happily engrossed in their archetypal myths and fantasies that their feet barely touch the ground; of Kleinians who spend so much of their life in the paranoid-schizoid position that they seem not to know of any other; and those, who shall be nameless, who so delight in playing creatively in their transitional space that the last thing they want to do is to cope with the hard work and conflict of living in the outside world.

I jest, of course, but there is truth in my words.

Ultimately, I suspect, whether or not we can cope with an eclectic approach depends upon the structure of our own personal inner world. If we have a basically obsessional temperament, what threatens us most is confusion and meaninglessness, and eclecticism can readily feed into that fear. If we have a more schizoid disposition, we can easily feel trapped and persecuted by a focused approach which allows no deviation. What at first sight appears to be a rational argument, actually impinges on our most basic fear, whether that be madness, or annihilation and non-being. No wonder passions run high!

In an ideal world, when considering a psychotherapeutic training, we should have a choice of approach, and we should be encouraged to think long and hard before committing ourselves. Where only one option is available, it is perhaps asking too much of some people that they live with this level of primitive anxiety

In a recent address to the Guild of Psychotherapists, Eleanor Armstrong-Perlman said:

'It has been one of the tragedies of the psychoanalytical world that there has been so much fragmentation. There has been a tendency to assume a monopoly of truth by some and a denial of the views of others. There has been a tendency to treat disagreement as 'unanalysed resistance' or an envious persecutory attack. Divisions have polarised around charismatic figures and have become confused with issues of loyalty and fidelity to a 'guru' mother or father figure. Such fragmentation can lead to a system which both accentuates and obscures difference.

The psychoanalytical world can be as schismatic as the early Christian church with the divisions between the faithful and the elect who can only be saved by being chosen by God, not by good works, and the heretics; never mind the unbaptised hordes of humanist or systems-theory pagans.'

She also spoke of '....the danger of trainings becoming analogous to religious indoctrination...where one is protected from exposure to those of different persuasions lest one should stray into error.' As she added 'In this scheme there is no model of tolerable confusion or uncertainty in which there can be gains from the exploration of difference.'

If Mrs. Armstrong-Perlman drew an analogy with the early Christian church, I was reminded of the conflicts of seventeenth-century England. At that time we had only recently given up burning people at the stake for holding unacceptable beliefs, and religious factionalism was rife. Some of the splinter groups of that time are still with us—the Baptists, the Congregationalists, the Quakers—though the passion is much attenuated. Others are long since gone—the Diggers, the Levellers, Ranters, Brownites and Fifth Monarchy Men—but at the time they were as vociferous, uncompromising and impervious to argument as yesterday's Communists or today's Militant Tendency. Poor Oliver Cromwell had thought the country would settle once King Charles was gone. Instead, parliamentary government was made impossible by the competing and irreconcilable passionate certainties of these groups with their excellent intentions; and if that wasn't enough, he had the Irish to contend with! No wonder that, for several generations afterwards, 'religious enthusiasm' was a term of disapproval.

William Penn, one of the first generation of Quakers, grew up during those turbulent years, being born just two years after the king lost his head. He was a gentleman by birth, and comes across in his writings as a man of considerable intelligence, charm and diplomacy. He used the latter to good effect in later life when he founded the new colony that came to be known as Pennsylvania, and it is to his credit that those early settlers negotiated a treaty and then lived in harmony with the native Indians for many years. It was in his middle age that he wrote the following words:

'The humble, meek, merciful, just, pious and devout souls are everywhere of one religion; and when death has taken off the mask they will know one another, though the diverse liveries they wear here makes them strangers.'

I find those words moving, particularly given their context; and as relevant now as they were then, and as relevant to the psychotherapeutic community as to the religious one. We have just about given up metaphorically burning our opponents at the stake. We still have our equivalent of the Ranters, the Levellers and Fifth Monarchy Men, and Ireland is with us still! Do we need to repeat history, within our own profession? And if we do, are we not in danger of bringing our enthusiasms into disrepute as thoroughly as those people did then.

I should like to end by telling a story which may already be familiar to you. It is a tale from the Sufi tradition, that mystical branch of Islam which presents such a very different face from the one we usually meet. It is called:

The Blind Men and the Elephant

There was a city and all its inhabitants were blind. A king with his entourage arrived near by; he brought his army and camped in the desert. He had a mighty elephant which he used in attack and to increase the people's awe.

The populace became eager to see the elephant, and some from amongst this blind community ran to find it. As they did not even know the form or shape of the elephant they groped sightlessly, gathering information by touching some part of it.

Each thought he knew something because he could feel a part.

When they returned to their fellow citizens, eager groups clustered around them, anxious to learn the truth.

They asked about the form, the shape of an elephant, and listened to all they were told.

The man whose hand had reached an ear said, 'It is a large, rough thing, wide and broad like a rug.'

And the one who felt the trunk said, 'I have the real facts about it. It is like a straight and hollow pipe, awful and destructive"

The one who had felt its feet and legs said, 'It is mighty and firm like a pillar.'

They fell into dispute with each other, and began to lay about them with their sticks. Finally they staggered off, each in a different direction.

Each had felt one part out of many, each had perceived it wrongly. All imagined something, something incorrect. No mind knew all. Knowledge is not the companion of the blind.

We are all blind; and we too grope in the dark. If we are ever to begin to comprehend that impressive and slightly comical animal, the human being, we need to share the little truth we have, and acknowledge its limitations. We need one another.

(1990)

Note

The story of the 'Blind Men and the Elephant' is a traditional Sufi tale. This early version was told by Hakim Sanai who died in 1150AD, and can be found in Idries Shah (1967).

Where Is Normality?

In the days of my psychotherapeutic innocence, I recall commenting to my analyst about my fantasy of a normal family. His wry response was that he had come to doubt if such an entity existed!

One of the many things our training gives us is an awareness of the unthinking assumptions we all carry within us as to what is normal. Of course, we all begin by believing that our own family is normal, that others think as we do, that our experience is much like everyone else's, that the world looks to others much as it does to us. If for any reason life feels uncomfortable, or we feel uncomfortable with our life, we tend to believe it is because there is something wrong with us, and this makes life hard for the child. It is one of the excitements of adolescence, when we enter a wider social world, to encounter difference. For those who leave home for university, this is one of the most important aspects of that experience.

Our unconscious assumptions are the bedrock of our personality—they make us what we are. Too much change too early, too much exposure to widely different expectations and value systems can undermine the developing sense of identity, leaving the individual unsure and tentative. We see this in children whose home has been disrupted by marital breakdown, and where a step-parent enters the scene. Whose values are they to internalise? It can be a problem, too, for children whose educational achievements take them out of the cultural environment in which they were reared. Parents who honestly wanted the best for their young come to feel that they have lost them as different value systems make their influence felt.

Our work with individuals takes us into this territory with a vengeance, and is familiar ground for us. Hopefully our own therapy has brought into consciousness those aspects of our personal experience which are ours and ours alone, and are irrelevant to the patient in front of us.

However, I feel we are only just beginning to address the wider social issues that multi-culturalism brings in its wake, not to mention globalisation. This challenges us not only on the individual level, but in the area of our basic cultural assumptions.

The issue of immigration can feel threatening because it confronts us with people who do not share our background. We cannot assume their thinking, their attitudes and beliefs are the same as ours. We are beginning to recognise that it is the children of immigrants who experience the most cultural difficulty, torn as they are between two different sets of customs and values. The recent film *Bend It Like Beckham* was a delightful story of an British Asian family struggling with just these issues.

Westerners who do business in Japan often find it difficult, because for the Japanese it is impolite to say 'no' to someone. They have elaborate circumlocutions to get around this social problem, and strangers can feel immensely frustrated if they expect a straight answer!

In a given culture, the space people habitually give each other varies considerably. If the 'other' stands too close, one can feel crowded; if a long way apart, he seems unfriendly. Misinterpretation is all too easy.

I recall a psychotherapist of my acquaintance who had lived and worked in India for some years. He said he had come to feel that, in the community he knew, the ego-boundary was not around the individual but around the family. This influenced all the psychodynamics of therapy, and had to be accepted and worked with. (He had found it hard!)

I wonder about the above-average incidence of schizophrenia within our indigenous Afro-Caribbean population. Are they really more vulnerable to this form of mental illness, or are the mental health professionals tending to diagnose as pathological, behaviour which is 'normal' within that group?

There have recently been a number of distressing cases of child cruelty among families originating from sub-Saharan Africa. The child has been ill-treated because it was believed to be possessed by evil spirits which needed to be exorcised. What was an acceptable response in the sub-group was both abhorrent and criminal to the host culture.

Too much naïveté in this domain can be disastrous as in the attempt by the USA to bring democracy to the Middle East, the assumption being that democracy is the only possible form of government for right-thinking people. Great Britain made similar attempts in the later days of empire. These political initiatives were never sustained because they were imposed from without, and we should have learned from history.

I suspect many of today's marital problems arise from the clash of unconscious assumptions. In the days when we tended to marry the boy or girl next door, or from the next village, one could take for granted a certain common stance on the basic business of living. Nowadays, we have so much social and geographical mobility, and are encouraged to believe that this is always positive, that we blind ourselves to the implications.

I was reminded of some of the more subtle aspects in which our unconscious assumptions can catch us out when learning of a failed therapy. This failure surprised me at first hearing since I understood that the professional concerned was competent and well-trained. However, further thought elucidated some of the tangle. There was a profound but hidden cultural clash.

Both parties were apparently British, white and middle-class.. However, one came from an upper-crust southern English milieu; the other from a family whose background and structure was Welsh. The one had learned independence early having gone away to boarding school, and been expected to stand on her own feet as soon as education ceased. The other had expectations of ongoing closeness and support as long as was needed, and felt under pressure to move in a direction which felt quite alien and unnatural. The end-result was an unmanageable negative transference, with the patient walking out.

It seems to me, coming as I do from a mixed Welsh/English background, that the Welsh family culture is a borderline one (see Masterson). That is, it tends to produce powerful matriarchs who cling to their children and make it difficult for them to separate, while the father is more often the gentle nurturing partner, the poet and dreamer. Whether this is the result of history—of being a defeated and occupied nation—or whether it is a long-established Celtic tradition, I am not sure. Was Boudicca unique? I doubt it.

Like all cultures, it has its good and its not-so-good aspects, but within its own boundaries it can work very well for its members. It is a culture which actually likes its children and nurtures their talent, with the result that it produces a disproportionate number of actors and singers, nurses and teachers, and the Palace of Westminster would be the poorer without its Celtic contingency.

I recall a street in the Valleys whose inhabitants went each year on holiday together, and had done so for twenty years. They loved this arrangement and couldn't envisage a better way of doing it!

But it is a very different culture from the adjacent English one, and the two do not always mix comfortably. In my experience, the Welshman has expectations of group support and solidarity which he does not find when he travels, and his ego-defences are ill-equipped to meet a fiercely individualistic and competitive culture. I recall more than one very able student who, on graduation, opted to stay in Wales rather than move to a better job across the border. His English teachers found this incomprehensible, but who can say where ultimately the greater happiness lay. Reciprocally, I have known many Welsh men and women who had crossed the border and couldn't wait to return. Whatever, those who successfully make the cultural transition still carry within them the assumptions, values and attitudes of their formative years, and these have their ongoing influence.

Does this family pattern constitute pathology, or is it simply another form of social organisation? Is the patient in my consulting room in dire need of help, or is he/she simply behaving in ways which are his/her cultural norm? It can, of course, be both. However, we need to be very sensitive to such subtle cultural differences if we are to be helpful and not damaging. To label certain patterns as pathological because they are not ours can be abusive.

(2005)

Our Perverse World

Each age produces its own cultural climate, and that climate creates characteristic artefacts which reflect the spirit of the time.

Living near Bath, I am very aware of the Georgian Age. Walking aound the city is rather like living in a film set. The rythmic pattern of the architecture is elegant and stylish—it is easy to imagine the folk of Jane Austen's era parading the streets in their elegant finery, and eying the matrimonial possibilities. If however, one walks aound to the back of these handsome terraces and crescents, it is a different story. The facades were built by speculative builders to a pattern; what was built behind was left to the new owners, and a higgledy-piggledy mess it tends to be. Moreover, weight-bearing walls can be as thin as five inches, so a survey is wise before purchase!

The wealth of Bath in its heyday was derived from the slave trade, with nearby Bristol the major port of call. However, the function of the spa was gambling, frivolity and the demonstration of conspicuous consumption, so this fact was out of mind in polite society. Jane Austen with her clarity of vision was well aware of the social contrasts during her stay here, and her tales make apparent the underlying superficiality and heartlessness of that society.

86

If I sound somewhat ambivalent about the charms of Bath, it is because I am. It was the Las Vegas of its day, and in my imagination something of that atmosphere still lingers. Nor have I ever been able to warm to the 'fine furniture' and pretty decor of that period. The words 'red hat and no knickers' comes into my mind—a childhood phrase denoting meretricious high style without substance!

The years of my growing belonged to an unmistakably depressive era. My immediate family were fortunate to have work, but we knew those who were unemployed for years during the Depression of the Thirties, and money was always tight. Economically the '39-'45 war brought relief to many, but the externals of life were cut to the bare bone. The prevailing ambience was of a dogged stoicism, 'stiff upper lip', 'Keep Smiling', 'Waste not, Want not', food rationing, clothing coupons, new clothes out of old curtains or parachute silk, shortage of fuel and dark streets. The end of the war brought little relief, and it was not until the Festival of Britain in 1951 that the atmosphere lightened. The artefacts of those years reflected the times. New (utility) furniture was spare and plain, made with the most basic of materials. (It was often very well designed bcause of the imposed constraints!) Clothes used minimal fabric, and fashion reflected the military influence—less than flattering to the female form! There was a tremendous upsurge in the popularity of classical music because the major orchestras and musicians toured the country, playing in halls they would never have considered under normal conditions; and the composer most heard was Beethoven. Life was serious, life was heroic, and Beethoven's music reflected that back to us. (By comparison, Mozart—today's favourite—was considered 'a bit light-weight!')

If my part of the world was in a depressive mode during those years, the wider world was exhibiting massive paranoid-schizoid phenomena in the nightmare societies of Nazi Germany and Stalin's Russia. In pre-Nazi Europe the arts reflected this regression to an earlier mode of functioning—I am thinking of the pain and disintegration expressed in the 'modern art' of Picasso and his generation, and of the development of atonal music which left mainstream composers out of fashion for two generations.

The post-war recovery plunged us into the hypomania of the Swinging Sixties, reminiscent of the post-1918 Flapper Era, but with the added bonus of sexual freedom granted by the Pill. Anything seemed possible, work was so readily available that for many young people it didn't seem worth the slog of long-term professional training, just as it didn't seem worthwhile to persist with long-term relationships once they became stale. Fashion was great fun, design of all kinds flourished, we built in the International Style ignoring the fact that what worked in the Mediterranean or Californian sun didn't quite stand up to our climate

Youth had a ball with little thought for the 'morrow, and coming down off the 'high' hit some hard. They never expected to be middle-aged!

Where are we now? My feeling is that we are living in a perverse society, using the term 'perverse' as defined by Chasseguet-Smirgel. I quote from the panel report on *Perversion* from the Barcelona Congress 1997 of the IPA (International Psycho-Analytic Association):

> 'Chasseguet-Smirgel... thinks that perversion constitutes a universal temptation of the human mind. This temptation is to attack reality by attempting to dissolve or deny all limits and boundaries and all differences. It wishes to rise above the ordinary laws of time and space. This process of confusion, of denial of specific attributes and the attempt at homogenisation becomes idealised and this forms what she terms the anal universe. The attack on separation, differentiation and naming, on specificity, leads to the construction of a substitute reality where anything can become anything else as a defense against the pain of having to accept one's relative place in reality. This is something that everyone must struggle with, that is, the giving up of narcissistic omnipotence and the maintenance of illusion, as well as the wish to own and control and use at will one's objects.

> The perverse act therefore seeks to create a new reality. It is also an attack on the mind and the functioning of the mind and on thinking.......
>
> .....To use Bion's term, this is an area of -K, where there is a breakdown of perception, knowledge and awareness.'

Under the guise of good liberal words and notions, I believe we have been engaging in a flight from reality. Under the guise of equality we have pretended that all people are much the same. Under the guise of equal opportunity we have refused to rcognise that different people have different levels of intelligence, different innate abilities, different gifts, and that these need to be met by appropriately tailored education. We have pretended that by changing colleges of technology into universities that they have achieved the same educational standing as the older universities. We have changed almost all our schools from streamed to comprehensive with a 'one model fits all' approach, and now wonder why we are woefully short of skilled craftsmen, engineers and scientists. We have discouraged competition between pupils, individually and collectively, ignoring past experience that boys, if not girls, love competing, and that this appeal to the male pecking order may be the only way to motivate them. Under the guise of feminism, we have pretended that men and women are only made different by social conditioning.. Under the guise of ageism, we try to deny that people do change over the years, for good and ill; that experience has value, and that declining physical resources needs to be accomodated. (Full-time work until seventy!?) We treat pop music as of equal value to the classical European canon, and raise to iconic status narcissistic personalities with minimal talent. Finally under the rubric of post-modernism, we put forward rational argument that there is no ultimate meaning in anything, thus wiping out history, theology and all that experience and tradition has given us.

Chasseguet-Smirrgel writes of how the pervert, in his inner world, reduces everything to an anal mess and muddle, like a child mixing together all the colours in its paint-box. The end-result is not the glory of the rainbow but a dirty formless mud. It is no coincidence that the Turner Prize of 1998 was given for an exhibition of elephant dung, or that other recent prizes have been for a pile of bricks, an unmade bed and the embalmed half-carcass of a calf. As always, our artists have captured the spirit of the age.

I noted, too, that in August 2001, Channel 5 television put out a programme in its *Real Sex* series on 'Whip-cracking sessions and a pageant for older strippers and dancers'. What would Lord Reith have said!*

The IPA report goes on to say while the social acceptibility of certain kinds of behaviour does vary at different times and between cultures, 'acceptable' does not necessarily imply 'harmless' either to the society or to the individual. To assert otherwise is to indulge in just that 'homogenisation' to which Chasseguet-Smirgel alludes.

I do believe that we are beginning to emerge from this phase. The excesses of the early feminists have been rejected and modified by their daughters and granddaughters as the realities of childcare have impinged..

There is a growing realisation that our education system is not delivering what was hoped for, and there are moves afoot to change it, while insisting that we are not turning back the clock. There is growing evidence that an approach which suits girls very well does not give boys what they need; that in a women-dominated profession, male teachers provide something much valued and needed.

Similarly, in the field of dietetics which has been a niche traditionally filled by women, we are beginning to realise that men and women thrive on distinctly different food—one which seems to reflect the Stone Age human specialisation into male hunters and women gatherers! Women love salad, but 'real men don't eat quiche!'

One could link, perhaps unkindly, the perverse spirit of our age with the cultural dominance of the USA since that nation was founded upon denial—from its basic tenet that all men are equal, to the expectation and encouragement that its immigrants forget about their countries of origin. While there was much wisdom in these attitudes in that they enabled a gathering of very disparate people to cohere into a nation, nontheless it denied certain basic human realities. Am I reading too much into the immediate present (2005-6) to link the beginnings of change in our own society to what I feel is a decline of American dominance in the world, and the current rise of Creation Theology** in their thinking?

The psychoanalyst Thomas Ogden, writing about psychic activity in the individual, believes that the different modes of functioning that belong to different stages of maturation—which he names as the autistic-contiguous, the paranoid-shizoid and the depressive— co-exist still in the adult. He sees the autistic-contiguous mode as providing the sensory floor of experience; the paranoid-schixoid the immediacy of concretely symbolised experience, while the depressive is the the principal medium through which symbolically mediated experience is generated. It is also the mode in which we have some historical perspective because of some sense of the passage of time. He believes that these different modes of functioning remain operative within the psyche. In his words: 'Experience is always generated between the poles represented by the ideal of the pure form of each of these modes.'

He suggests that psychopathology can be understood as forms of collapse in the equilibrium between these three modes. Collapse towards the autistic-contiguous pole and we become trapped in 'the machine-like tyranny of attempted sensory-based escape from the terror of formless dread, by means of reliance on rigid autistic defenses.' Collapse towards the paranoid-schizoid pole and we become trapped in 'a non-subjective world of thoughts and feelings experienced in terms of frightening and protective things that simply happen, and that cannot be thought about or interpreted.' Collapse in the direction of the depressive pole involves 'a form of isolation from one's bodily sensations, and from the immediacy of one's lived experience, leaving one devoid of spontaneity and aliveness.'

While he is here writing about the individual, I suspect similar processes are at work in the wider social scene.

One could understand the nineteenth century Evangelical Movement as society's collapse in the direction of the depressive pole. We have only just recovered from 'the isolation from one's bodily sensations, and from the immediacy of one's lived experience.' As a society, having in the last forty years recovered our spontaneity and aliveness, none of us would want to go back to the inhibitions and repressions of the late nineteenth and early twentieth centuries.

My sense is that we have been tending towards collapse in the direction of the autistic-contiguous pole, desperately seeking sensory-based satisfactions while at the same time many of us choose to live alone because that is the best we can manage. We get together with others to 'have fun' or sex, but spend much of the rest of our lives relating to a computer, a television set or driving vast distances in cars. Perhaps the current ubiquity of the mobile phone is a plus factor after all. It is human contact of a kind, if only at a distance!

What Freud termed' polymorphous perverse sexuality'—that very early, unfocused expression of sensory excitement in the normal infant—would seem to belong to that phase of development when we move from the autistic-contiguous mode into the paranoid-schizoid one. Is one element in the generation of perverse behaviour in the adult a regression back to that primitive level of experience?

Where next? Perverse behaviour was rampant in the late days of Rome, before the barbarians flooded into the Western half of the Empire, and the centre of power moved to Byzantium. It was also widespread amongst the upper classes in the late Georgian and Regency period, and it would seem to be in reaction to such behaviour that the nineteenth century Evangelical Movement took such rapid hold. It was a feature of the Weimar Republic if Christopher Isherwood's lightly fictionalised account is to be believed. Would the Nazi ideology have had the appeal it did except in reaction to that which preceded it?

A certain authoritianism is creeping into our political and judicial system, and we are allowing it because the alternative anarchy and destruction which terrorism threatens feels like a worse alternative. Perhaps some corrective is necessary, but the trend has its dangers. However, while Church membership is still in decline, there is an upsurge in spirituality of various kinds as people search for a

Weltanschauung which gives them a framework for creative living. Retail therapy is losing some of its appeal as the cost of housing weighs heavy, and the pension crisis intrudes. The threat of climate change can no longer be ignored. Reality is impinging, and demands to be addressed.

I have no slick answers, only questions. I am just noting a certain pricking in my thumbs, an unease as I scent possible dangers ahead. 'Truth is the daughter of time', but the timespan of a human life is short, and long-term trends are obscure. What we all need, as we have always needed, is a perspective, a faith if you like, that will carry us through the dark times and the good.

Sir John, later Lord, Reith was the first Director-General of the BBC. He did an excellent job for his young organisation in many ways. However, he was a Highland Scot from a Calvinist background and of a somewhat dour temperament, and his firm hand on programme content reflected his own perspective.

**Creation Theology. Currently widespread in the US, especially amongst Christians holding Fundamentalist beliefs. A denial of Darwinian evolution, and an explanation of the pre-history of our world in terms of special creation by the Deity.*

(2005)

Words & Before Words

There are, I know, colleagues in the psychotherapy/ psychoanalysis domain for whom words are paramount. I regard them with awe. They make me aware that there are subtleties of communication which pass me by. Also, since they often come from a background in philosophy and my own excursions into this field of intellectual activity have been dismally unsuccessful (I rarely get beyond page three of any book I have tackled!), I have little hope of ever matching their insight. However I have to confess that there is a part of me that is unconvinced.

My own attitude to words is ambivalent. I love the written word, whether in prose or poetry, and enjoy playing in that space. The spoken word is another matter. Words can lie as much as communicate. They can be used to deny, to evade, to obfuscate and mislead. So, of course, can the written word, but in reading one has the time and opportunity to reflect and judge.

Undoubtedly my attitudes reflect my own personal experience. I grew up in an era when lying to children was the norm, especially about matters of sex, death and adult relationships - all for the children's good, of course. To be fair, my own parents were more honest than many. At the same time, I was acutely sensitive to the routine attempts to manipulate me on various issues when obedience was required. (I must have been a tiresome child!) The result was that I found silence a more powerful weapon and defensive strategy than words. I also learned to 'listen' to emotional atmosphere.

This background proved valuable when it came to relating to those patients who, in increasing numbers, presented with borderline constellations. So much of the work was about exploring the pre-oedipal, pre-verbal period of their development. While words had eventually to be found so that they could think about their experiences, it was vital not to 'jump the gun' and interpret too soon. Words could all too easily be felt as intrusive, wrecking the mood and dissipating the emotional charge of the session. Since these patients were often incapable of defending themselves in this situation as it represented the repetition of an old pattern, it was all too easy for one's enthusiasm to take the therapy in entirely the wrong direction.

I found Christopher Bollas' comments on mood very helpful and confirming. Thomas Ogden's conceptualisation of the early autistic-contiguous stage of development was a valuable insight, and I used it with dramatic success with a highly intelligent but extremely difficult patient when an interpretation based on Ogden's perspective marked a turning-point in a therapy close to failure.

Alessandra Pontielli's research into post-natal and foetal life confirmed my own intuition that these very early experiences are formative; and while birth trauma has been given undue weight in some circles as the primary explanation of all mental disturbance, nontheless it is our first experience of a major transition and I suspect sets the tone for how we cope with subsequent transitions in life.

But perhaps the author who taught me most in this field was Harold Searles. His work with psychotic patients, and the sensitivity and humility he brought to it are unequalled in my experience. His understanding of the use of the non-verbal non-personal world by these very damaged patients enlarged my comprehension immeasurably.

Thus it was with interest that a recent article in the *International Journal of Psychoanalysis* by Mauro Mancia alerted me to the contribution that is currently being made by neuroscience to the understanding of our earliest experience.

Neuroscientists recognise two kinds of memory systems. The first is *explicit memory* which can be retrieved consciously and verbalised. It concerns specific events in one's life and allows one to give meaning to the recollection of experience. It is explicit memory that we work with as we enable patients to reconstruct their personal history. Research with brain-damaged patients using scanning techniques has enabled us to learn which parts of the brain are involved in the storage and retrieval of explicit memory. What is also interesting is that where brain damage has resulted in amnesia such that individuals cannot recall events of the previous day, nontheless they can dream about them when asleep.

The second kind of memory - *implicit memory* - by contrast is not conscious and contains data that can be neither remembered nor verbalised. It is involved in the learning of certain basic skills (*priming* and *procedural memory*), and also in *emotive and affective memory*. This latter concerns the emotional experiences (including the defences and phantasies) linked to the first relations of the child with its environment and particularly its mother. It seems likely that this memory is also linked to the experience of the foetus in the womb during the later stages of gestation. The mother's rhythms, and in particular her voice 'constitute a pattern of continuity, rhythm and musicality around which the first representations of the infant are organised.'

It seems that it is now generally accepted in neuro-scientific circles that the sensori-motor experiences of the foetus can be memorised. So also can the voice of the mother, and when re-experienced particularly during breast-feeding can influence the heart-rate and even the suction rate of the infant. At this early stage the child is very sensitive to the intonation and rhythm of the maternal language, and begins to reproduce it (as babble) from about six months of age.

Explicit memory, which is capable of repression, depends on the functioning of the hippocampus. However, this part of the brain is not yet mature in early infancy. The organisation of implicit memory appears to be the function of the amygdaloid nuclei which mature earlier. (For someone who, as a medical student fifty-odd years ago, dissected these structures within the brain but at a time when we had little knowledge of their function, this is exciting stuff!) It is therefore suggested that these earliest forms of memory can only be stored as implicit memory and are not capable of repression. Hence we have an early unrepressed unconscious core of the self.

It seems that there is still much work to be done to understand the full complexity of the neural networks and the different parts of the brain involved in the different types of memory. However, enough is now accepted which throws some very interesting light upon our own clinical experience.

Even more startling is the work at the micro-biological level (Rose 1992; Kandel 1999) which suggests that there is a genetic memory located in chromosomal DNA, and that relational and social factors can exert action on the brain, modifying permanently the function of the genes. In other words, we now have a mechanism to explain how psychic trauma can get in to the psychosomatic domain. It also revives the long-discredited notion of the inheritance of acquired characteristics. 'Culture' can become 'nature'!

This understanding of implicit memory sheds light on many aspects of our work, on the quality of the patient/therapist relationship; on the transferential/counter-transferential emotions that get stirred which may have little relationship to the overt content of the sessions; on the quality of 'mood' to which Bollas alerts us; on how we use our voice as distinct from the actual words we choose; on our understanding and interpretation of dreams which can give shape to our most archaic experiences; on the whole realm of music and its meaning for us.

This pre-verbal pre-symbolic world of the infant has always been with us in the consulting room. Now the neuro-scientists are giving us the concepts, the tools with which to think about it, and which hopefully will enable us to bring it into the verbal domain.

Words may be a mixed blessing, but they are indeed vital tools of our trade, and in the history of our species a major human achievement!

(2006)

The Spiritual Dimension

*

Patterns: Some Random Thoughts On Psychotherapy & Spirituality

Psychotherapy and spirituality can be seen as deriving from the same impulse—the need for meaning. People are pattern seekers and pattern makers. The very young neonate, so the psychologists tell us, reacts to three dots in the shape of an inverted triangle as if it were a human face. Later we hear the sound of the sea as we hold a sea-shell to our ears, and we strain to hear voices in so-called 'white noise' which contains absolutely no information whatsoever.

Much of the art of the mother is to bring the world to the infant in such a way that it makes sense to the child, as well as protecting it from massive sensory experience which might overwhelm its capacity to process that experience. In doing so, the mother lays down the foundation of future mental health. One could view mental ill-health as a failure in this domain. If total, then we have madness; if partial we see splitting and repression and all the subsequent repercussions as the individual attempts to meet the challenges of life with impaired ability. (Of course, I am over-simplifying grossly.)

One can see human development as an ongoing process of experiencing the world, and making sense of and integrating that experience. It even goes on while we are asleep. It is never complete and continues while we have life.

Psychotherapy encompasses many kinds of experience—the abreaction of emotion, the recall of forgotten memories, a new and different kind of relationship—but a crucial aspect is the creation by the patient of a coherent narrative of his/her life. The emergence of previously unconscious material, the interpretations offered by the therapist, the making of connections and associations, all enable a new pattern to emerge—a pattern which makes sense in a way it never previously did. This is comforting in itself, but it is more than that. It is transforming. It brings with it confidence and energy for living.

I have never worked with a patient over a long period of time—I am talking here in terms of years—without them finally beginning to ask the ultimate questions. What is life all about? What is *my* life all about? What is the point of it all? Of all this suffering?

Whether or not it is framed in religious terms depends on the patient's previous frame of reference. Sometimes they can use religious words and imagery, sometimes not. It seems irrelevant to the urge to find some kind of framework or Weltanschauung in which they can find ultimate meaning.

There are of course other aspects of the spiritual journey which may or may not have parallels in the psychotherapeutic one. The search for some kind of certainty, something or Someone which never changes, raises all kind of questions for the therapist. Some of us would be inclined to interpret it as a defence against the threat of inner chaos and disintegration, although one has to admit that there are those professionals in our field who behave as if they have the definitive answers. In mitigation, I recall Haya Oakley in her 1995 Public Lecture to the Severnside Institute for Psychotherapy saying that few people have the internal stability and maturity to live in the face of total uncertainty. An explicit religious faith can be very helpful in coping with the existential anxieties around the unknown and unknowable.

102

The spiritual journey can also encompass a desire for the experience of the numinous, the transcendent. Although not emphasised in much conventional Christianity outside the writings of the mystics (and considered rather suspect in some religious circles) it is, as the 35-year long researches of the Alister Hardy Society* have found, so widespread as to be probably a universal experience. As psychotherapists, we can attempt to explain it as a memory of life in the womb, or of a very early infantile state before any sense of the Self and Other has developed—a time when we felt alive and contained, the world perfectly attuned to our needs. (I am reminded here of the words of Henry Vaughan the Silurist, 'Prayer is the world in tune.')

Whatever, when people feel safe enough to talk about it, it is frequently described as having immense value and transformative power.

There is a social element to this pattern seeking. What binds together a social group, a community, a nation, is some kind of framework of reference in common. There is a common history, a common language, a common religion, a common ethical and legal code. Where these do not exist, there has to be a concerted attempt to create them as happened in the USA during its formative years. Where there are communities which have too few of these factors in common, then there are social splits and tensions and disruptions. We have seen these chronically in Northern Ireland and in the Balkans.

In Great Britain today, we have a potentially difficult situation as certain minority groups with a very different Weltanschauung to the prevalent post-Christian one become more numerous. We have the task of integrating Islam with our native culture, and that represents a major social challenge since the pattern of thinking, the interpretation of basic human experience, is so different, with such a different history.

I am aware that the current problems in our society arise from a perverted version of Islam, but of course all societies have their pathological elements. We learn over time to manage our own pathological individuals, after a fashion, if not very successfully.

When there develops more than one kind of social perversion, it becomes more difficult to contain and manage these elements, and injustices are more likely to occur.

(2005)

Sir Alister Hardy FRS was Professor of Marine Biology at Oxford, and began his research into religious experience in 1969 as a retirement exercise, feeling that religious experience was too summarily dismissed by the scientific community of the time.

The Alister Hardy Society can now be contacted at The Department of Theology & Religious Studies, University of Wales, Lampeter, Ceredigion SA48 7ED.

It has an annual conference, local meetings, and a publication and cassette list.

What is Human?

All of us have a life task, to make something out of what we have been given – 'given' in the sense of our innate endowment, our physical body with its strengths and limitations, our particular mix of intelligence and talents; 'given' in the sense of what we acquire from our family culture, the social milieu of our early years, the cultural values which surround us, explicit and implicit, at all stages of our journey. At the beginning, such is our need to believe that our parents are good that we do our best to accept what we are given, and see our family as normal and much like everyone else's. In adolescence, we rebel, see faults and limitations, and are ready to make the world anew. Then we begin selecting what is significant, what has meaning for us, begin integrating into some kind of coherent whole our history to date with the experiences life brings us.

There have been times when I felt life was a matter of staggering from one crisis to another! If not crisis, then certainly challenge. The ordinary transitions—marriage, children, ageing, moving house, changing jobs—throw up all sorts of feelings; depths of confusion and vulnerability, of uncertainty, doubt and sadness never dreamed of in our arrogant youth, as well as unexpected satisfactions, joys and the occasional burst of ecstasy.

And each challenge and response changes our perspective on what has gone before, makes us examine afresh what is important to us, modifies our sense of values; and in doing so we change, and the world we create around us is also subtly changed.

The Beginnings of Being

Already, I am sharing something about the way I see the world—that I have an essentially developmental perspective of the human personality, rooted in the biological realities; that I see the world as in a state of flux, of becoming; that I believe we all do contribute, in however small a way, to the world that is coming into being.

These are not new ideas. Teilhard de Chardin formulated them in the 20th century, and the scientific theory of complexity is providing us with an even more recent perspective. The language differs, but the underlying message is the same. We live in a world in the process of creation, and we are part of that creation. We need to come to terms with that in all its glory and limitations if we are ever to know who we really are.

Ultimately, we cannot 'know', cannot totally understand the universe since we are inside the system. Only God can hold the universe in his hand like a nut, as Julian of Norwich so beautifully expressed it. We can no more know about eternity than a chicken in the egg or a child in the womb can know about the world outside. We can only have faith, can hang on to the belief that it all makes sense ultimately. Meanwhile, we must wait in what is the right place for us, at our stage of development, and work at the task in hand until it is time to move on. For all of us here, that task is coming to terms with our own incarnation.

What are the limitations of incarnation? One stems from intellectual cleverness—we have literally grown large heads! This makes birth a more difficult process for both infant and mother than in other animals. *

A second stems from the fact that at birth we are very immature, singularly helpless and vulnerable. We have yet to acquire much of the basic programming we need in order to develop. Whereas

106

many species are born with much of their programming in-built—
what we call their instinctual endowment—for us only some of it
comes with our genetic package. A large part is acquired during the
first two years of life—and that part hard to modify once installed,
and then only with great pain. It is not coincidental that our heads
—our brains—continue to grow during those two years, and only
then do the fontanelles close and the cranial bones finally fuse.

As a species, we are slow growing to maturity, and during that
long period we still require protection and care, which puts great
burdens on those doing the caring.

We are putting an intolerable strain upon today's young women—
let me amend that statement: they are putting an intolerable strain
upon themselves—by trying to adopt essentially masculine
working patterns and expectations whilst also wanting to raise
children. As for men, the pressure to make work their priority can
be hard to resist, yet it diverts them from their primary task with
crucial consequences.

And yes, I know that many young couples must both work to
survive financially, but what is that saying about our society? And
what of the consequences? I was interested in a recent survey by an
Englishwoman who had lived in New York for some years, a
clinical psychologist working with child drug abusers. She was
interested in the factors which correlated with drug abuse; and
examined first the obvious parameters of class, colour, location,
finance etc. To her surprise she found that none of them seemed
significant. The one factor which did correlate directly was the
amount of time the drug-abusing child spent alone. She
commented 'In New York having children is treated as like having
a dog or a boat—a personal indulgence and no business of the
community at large'. We follow that pattern at our peril.

These are basic, obvious matters—yet how hard it is to remain
aware of them and the ensuing implications for the way we live,
the way we order our society, and in particular, the way we
organise work and family life.

Family Matrix

Back to our vulnerable infant. Winnicott said that there was no such thing as a baby, since no baby could be considered a viable entity apart from its mother or mother-substitute. I go further and claim that there is no such thing as a mother and child—since that unit can only function properly within a social matrix which supports its primary task. That social matrix has traditionally been the family. At times other arrangements have been suggested, even tried, the most recent being the Israeli kibbutzim, but none has been successful enough to last.

Size and shape of families have varied greatly with history, culture, geographical situation and, above all, economic realities. Religious and political sanctions reflect, quite as much as create, acceptable attitudes. Thus, where the living is hard, people tend to marry late, and often die relatively young, so that the three generation extended family is uncommon.

Polygamy occurs where land is plentiful but labour scarce. Several wives gives the one man a pool of labour—his wives and children —who can successfully work his land. By contrast, polyandry occurs where land is scarce but labour plentiful. By several brothers sharing one wife, they are able to hold on to their land and avoid it fragmenting into economically non-viable units.

The development of our present nuclear family came with the industrial revolution, which drew unattached young people into the towns. Without the support of extended family, they developed their own culture, which put a gulf between them and the parents. We have seen a comparable development in recent times, with the enormous social and geographical mobility of the post-war era, and the consequences of higher education for people of working-class origins.

Developmentally, what do we need by way of family? In this gathering I hardly need expound the significance of the mothering function. Most of you have looked at that in depth in your seminars. Perhaps I can add just a few comments from my own perspective.

Firstly, the most important qualities of infant care seem to be continuity and consistency. It is in the basic repetitive rhythm of physical care that the child gets some sense of its own physical boundaries, of being contained within its own skin; so that its feelings and its excitement do not tear it apart; of living in a world that has some pattern to it, that makes sense, that can be understood. It is in this first relationship that the infant learns to be comfortable in relationship to another (the beginning of sociability as opposed to schizoid or autistic isolation); learns to play (the beginning of all cultural activities); and learns to be alone, first in the presence of another, and then, by internalising that experience, to be comfortably alone with itself.

An important part of the mother's function is to bring the world to the child in a way that makes sense, in a way stimulating enough to be interesting, yet not so stimulating that the infant is overwhelmed. Reflected in their mother's eyes, babies learn who they, whether they are acceptable, interesting, of value, loved, or whether they are not worth responding to; and hence, whether life is worth the effort of living or not.

These are fundamental things that mothers do without knowing they are doing them, because their own mothers did them. What it does require is the capacity of the mother to give herself to that primary maternal pre-occupation for a time, and for the social matrix in which she functions to allow her to do so. She cannot do it harassed by anxious relatives or well-meaning but intrusive professionals, or if her husband feels neglected and becomes demanding, or if she has to worry about money. This is a crucial period which lasts a very short time. It needs to be protected and sanctioned.

Fatherhood

If a baby has to have a mother to survive, it needs a father in order to develop. By father, I mean someone who fulfils the fathering function—initially, someone who can support the mother, providing a stable, contained environment which enables her to function well during those crucial early days and weeks, and who creates a barrier between the mother-infant couple and the demands of the outside world. It does not have to be the woman's mate or the baby's father. Where the man is absent, away at war or at business (much the same thing!) it is often older women in the family who fill the breach. But where the man is present and fulfils this function well, it enormously strengthens the parental bond, which augurs well for the future health of the family. Where the man fails at this point because of other pressures, personal immaturity or whatever, the woman feels let down and experiences resentment of a kind from which it is difficult to recover. It is a crucial point in the marriage.

The fathering role changes in line with the child's development, paralleling change in the mother's function. Come the toddler stage and the beginning of separation /individuation, roughly 18 months to 3 years, the father has again a crucial function in facilitating that separation between mother and child which is vital to the child's mental health. He does it in part by involving himself more with the child—and most men relate more readily to the child after babyhood. He provides the child with different feedback as to who it is, so they are not trapped within the single perspective of their relationship with Mother. He provides the sense of other people, another world out there to which the child can aspire—a world of different experiences and values. At the same time, he signals to the mother that she is not just a mother, and that the mothering role has to change, to be gradually let go and transformed into something else, at least for this baby. Some mothers welcome this change, themselves more at ease with the older child; others find such satisfaction in a small baby that it is difficult to move on, and they cling to early symbiotic modes of relating longer than appropriate, damaging the child's growth. It needs a father who is there, and firmly there as a separate personality, for the child to surmount this particular hurdle.

Having negotiated this phase, the father is then available to the child as an alternative source of strength and power in the family— we are into the family triangle, the constellation we call the Oedipus complex. The primitive burgeoning of what later will be seen more clearly as sexuality appears with as much passion as in its later manifestations. Providing that the setting is safe enough for

110

the child to feel free to show its feelings—which means, if the parents feel comfortable with their own sexuality—then it can be quite delightful to watch the excitement of the small daughter when her Daddy comes home, and observe their horse-play together. This is when she learns to flirt with the opposite sex. Similarly, provided the little boy has safely emerged from early symbiotic closeness with mother, and has no doubt about his own separateness, he is free to discover her as an erotic object, and himself as capable of evoking that special kind of interest from a person of the other sex.

It is not all plain sailing. The ambivalence, even downright negativism, towards the parent of the same sex can be hard to bear. It can be infuriating for the woman who has put up with a tiresome, difficult small daughter having tantrums all day, to see her child transformed into a delightful baggage the moment Daddy appears through the door. Similarly, the father who has looked forward to having another small male in the family with whom to share boyhood interests has to have patience to bear the hostile rejection which is his lot during this phase. If he can, he will be rewarded as his son decides that 'if you can't beat 'em, join 'em', and then increasingly identifies with him.

An important fathering task at this stage is to provide a model of what it is to be a man, and above all an effective man, who can cope out there in the world, and can cope within the home, who can manage the child's aggression and sexuality, who can manage his own, and who can manage the mother as well. In other words, he needs to provide a model of acceptable authority.

It's a tall order! The wonder is that we manage family dynamics as well as we do. The world out there is often unhelpful, if not actively hostile, to our attempts to do a good job of parenting. Men are under the most acute pressure to succeed in their work at the same time as they are rearing their small children—assuming they have work to go to. Without a job, it is hard for them not to feel devalued, in which case their role is undermined. Insofar as women choose, or increasingly have to follow the male working model, they have the same problem. If they are so fortunate as not to be under that kind of financial compulsion, they are often so unsupported and lonely in the home that it seems easier to capitulate, join the workforce and make such provision for the child as one can find.

My professional hackles rise when I hear politicians pontificating about alternative childcare, which all too often means inferior child care. I do not wish to be judgmental; individuals do the best they can in the circumstances in which they find themselves. But social attitudes do influence the decisions people take at turning points in their lives, and I feel most strongly that we are losing sight of fundamental issues about child development. It is the children who suffer first, but subsequently we all suffer, having to live with the casualties in our society, violence, the drug problem, marital breakdown, child abuse and so on.

I am digressing. Back to fathering. As I have defined it, can it only be done by the biological father? Can it only be done by a man? That first function, of putting a protective barrier around the mother-infant unit, can be done, and quite often is, by others when the men are absent.

That second function, of gently encouraging the separation of mother and child, and luring the child into the wider world, again is not a gender-linked function. However, I think it is a role more difficult for someone other than father to take. Others might mutter behind mother's back, or even to her face, that perhaps she is being over-protective or over-involved, but it is rare for anyone to have the emotional power for mother and child that her man has, and others are reluctant to intervene. (Sometimes fathers do fail at this point, leaving the child to struggle unsupported with the separation/individuation issue. The consequences may not be seen until the threshold of adulthood, when the child has trouble leaving home and making the transition to independence.)

The subsequent fathering roles seem inextricably linked to gender. It is only a man who can function as the heterosexual object for the daughter and the rival to the son. It is only a man who can provide a model for the small boy of how to be a man, and only a man who can teach the little girl how to be a woman in relation to a man. Does it have to be the biological father? No, of course not. It may be stepfather, uncle or grandfather. It may be a neighbour or family friend (though that can have its dangers, as we are all aware at present with so much publicity around child abuse). Under some circumstances these normally subsidiary figures play a vital role .

It is as if children have some innate knowledge of what and who they need in order to grow, and search around in their environment for the figure who most nearly fulfils that blueprint.

Anthropologists tell us that there are some cultures where the chief man in a woman's life is not her husband but her brother, and it is he, not the biological father, who performs the fathering function. There are many variations on the theme; what seems to be important is that there is someone who functions in this capacity and that everyone understands who it is, that there is some innate stability in the culture, that it makes sense to the actors in the drama.

I have spent some time talking about fathers because I believe that much of our current social pathology has its roots in the lack of adequate fathering in our society; and that this lack of adequate fathering can be traced back to the ravages of the 1914-18 war when so many young men were killed in battle. The result was a generation of boys brought up without any adequate model of maleness, by women who were not in an ongoing relationship with a man. Such boys were often put into a false position, trying to compensate for the lost man while subject to the anxiety that that loss occasioned. They in turn did not know how to father adequately, or indeed how to relate in a mutually satisfying way to their womenfolk. I suspect that one—only one—of the roots of feminism lies here, and that feminism in its turn has tended to undermine the father's sense of his role in the family—but I will leave that thought with you, and simply comment that as a society we have paid, and continue to pay, a terrible price for the two European wars of the twentieth century.

A short glance at mothering, a longer look at fathering. Let us try to put our basic human needs into a wider context.

Significant Others

Ideally we need to be welcomed into the world from the beginning, and to have a place to come into. We need parents mature enough to put aside their own agendas in order to give their infant what it needs, but who have enough personal self-esteem to claim back their lives when it becomes appropriate to do so.

I believe that ideally we need an extended family who can share the burden of parenthood, and function as alternate sources of nurture and models of being. We need significant others in the adult world to whom we can turn when we have fallen out with our family, or when we are sick of the sight of the lot of them and feel thoroughly misunderstood and hard done by. One of the worst things about having only one parent is that one cannot afford to have a proper row, and without that experience how can we properly learn to manage our aggression.

We need others, outside the family, as well as within, to recognise our talents and abilities and nurture them, people from whom we learn, and who initiate us into the adult world of work. And, as adults, we need work to give us not only a livelihood but a place in the wider society, status, a role which gives structure and meaning to our lives. We need to feel we have a contribution to make, and that it is valued.

And at this point, we should ask what is happening in our society and what we are doing about it. The currently high level of unemployment is never going to drop back to previous levels, because many kinds of work are disappearing. Yet those who have work are working longer and harder than ever before. Should we not be thinking seriously about reducing the length of the working week? Isn't it ridiculous to be raising the age of retirement of women to that of men, instead of vice versa? How do we cope with a fall in remuneration for some if work is spread more evenly? Yet to fail to tackle these questions is to produce a disaffected under-class to whom we give no status, no self-respect, no life structure. That is trouble going somewhere to happen.

If we need to work, we also need to play; and play needs space. In the beginning it needs space between mother and child—what Winnicott calls transitional space, the forerunner of all creative thinking as well as shared cultural activities. The growing child needs space, and I find it sad that our society at present makes it less safe for children to play than when I was young. They cannot play in the streets because there is too much traffic. It no longer feels safe to allow them to play out of sight and hearing of their caretakers. We cannot even allow them to walk alone to school. That is a real loss for the child, and the constraints can feel oppressive. They no longer learn skills of coping on their own until much later in life, and when they are of an age to insist on privacy their 'play' can break out with a vengeance.

As adults too we need to play. We need to play by involving ourselves in joint social activities—and how hard that can be, given the excessively long working hours of many of us. We need to play sexually to keep our relationships in good heart—and not just on our fortnight's annual holiday in the sun. We need to play theologically—to find enough safe places from which to explore the deeper meanings of our busy lives, our shadow side, to contemplate 'the madness of sane men', the darker side of God, to ask the ultimate questions, to pray. Some go on retreats, some come to Clinical Theology conferences(!), others find what they need in therapy or counselling. These opportunities can be vital to us, and I look back with deep gratitude to some of the people I shared such events with, and whose generosity made them possible

And when we fail our children, as inevitably we do, because we are not perfect, and because outside events are not under our control, and when also we fail our fellow adults, it is vitally important that we acknowledge that failure. Because at some level, however it may be denied, the other person knows they have been failed. They may not be able to put it into words, may not even know in what area of need they have been deprived, but they feel it; and at that point something is arrested, stops growing, becomes soured. When the failure is acknowledged, the feelings can be felt, words can be put to them, it becomes possible to think about what has happened and to mourn. With mourning comes the possibility of forgiveness, of reparation and new growth.

Boundary Confusion

I would like at this point to talk briefly about two subjects which are areas of growing understanding in my own professional field

115

and which I see as two of our major contemporary social sins. Both arise from early developmental failure.

One is Narcissism; and by this I do not mean the proper self-regard we all need to feel of value, but something more destructive and insidious. It was summed up for me in a remark made by Margaret Thatcher. What she said was to the effect that 'there is no such thing as society, there are only individuals'. I cannot know what she had in mind when she uttered those words, and I am not wishing to deny her very considerable talents and ability. However, I hear that remark as of someone deeply out of touch with her own dependency needs, with the dependency we all have upon each other in our complex society, and someone lacking the empathy needed to feel with another. There are many such people in our society, and the ambience of recent years has tended to foster such attitudes. They are often 'successful' and charismatic, and a disaster in their personal relationships. To try for a warm and intimate relationship with such a person is to subject oneself to endless deprivation and frustration, since they are notoriously low on insight. Insofar as crude political terminology has any value, and like most stereotypes it represents a certain truth, I would see narcissism as the sin of the political Right.

The sin of the political Left I see as Perversion. Now I am using that word in a technical sense, and what I mean by perversion is the denial of difference. That is not just my personal idiosyncratic use of the word. If you want its provenance, the French psychoanalyst Janine Chasseguet-Smirgel used it in her book on *Creativity and Perversion*, in 1984, and a more accessible read is a recent book called *Female Perversion* by Louise Kaplan.

The central argument is the same—that the root of perversion is the denial of difference; of the difference between the sexes, of the difference between the generations, of the difference between people of different background and tradition.

Now we all have perverse tendencies within us. We enjoy playing around with the boundaries, particularly during adolescence when we are exploring who we might be. We enjoy cross-dressing, trying out for size the clothes, attributes, fantasies even, of the other sex. We develop passionate relationships with quite 'unsuitable' people, not infrequently fall in love with someone much older than ourselves. It is appropriate to that age group, and if it is sometimes alarming to the staid onlooker, it can also be quite charming. It is, however, a phase that naturally has an end.

A Hindu concept describes four different stages of life, each with its appropriate duties and concerns. The responsibility and fundamental concern of the householder stage, more or less corresponding with mature adulthood, is to create and maintain structures—personal, family and social. If behaviour which I have just been describing, appropriate to the adolescent (student) phase, is carried on into adulthood, it can be destructive to both the individual and their nearest and dearest.

Maybe we need our anarchic personalities, our rebels who challenge established values, and would be dull and imaginatively poorer without them. However, any society can only afford to carry a limited number of such people, and we can only make creative use of them if they are contained within a stable social structure. The romanticisation of the rebel, current for some decades, has led us into a schizoid cul-de-sac in the arts, an explosion of perverse material in the media, and the uncontained acting-out of phantasy among the less well-balanced in our society.

In psychodynamic terms, the denial of difference has its origins in the failure of the growing child to cope with the family triangle. It is the reaction of the child who actively refuses to come to terms with the fact that he cannot be a proper mate for his mother, that she cannot marry her father. Why this is such a problem for some children and not others is a wider and more complex question.

The reality is that the sexes are different, and in my experience on the obstetric wards of a hospital, they are different from the moment of birth. (I may say that this was a surprise to me—it was not what I expected.) Similarly age is significant. We live in time and belong to a particular epoch. The preoccupations, the significant events, the idols, the dominant attitudes are different for different generations. There is a sense in which they live in different worlds.

117

Children are not appropriate sexual partners for adults, and clinical experience suggests that most are profoundly damaged if they are trapped into that false role.

Similarly, our background, whatever it is, does shape us. We may grow from it, grow away from it, but we shall never be the same as if we had grown from different roots.

It is easy to see, at the social level, how much of this denial came into being. After the 1939-45 war there was a powerful urge among the people of this country, particularly amongst returning servicemen, their perspectives immensely broadened, to do away with the old class distinctions and re-form society in a more flexible pattern.

Similarly the role of women changed, and much former discrimination was no longer acceptable. There has been tremendous loosening up of attitudes which restricted and imprisoned people in unnecessary and destructive ways, and one can only welcome these changes.

Having said that, there is a whole world between rejecting discrimination and denying difference. There are real differences between people, and we need to accept that fact, and indeed to celebrate it. We need the richness it brings. To deny the reality is to produce a nasty muddle and mess in which individuals get badly hurt and our social morality decays.

To relate these conditions back to our psychodynamic perspective, the roots of both narcissism and perversion are in early developmental failure. The narcissist has lost trust in human relationships and attempts to protect himself from further hurt by retreating into a pseudo self-sufficiency. It can look like an enviable independence; the reality is that by rejecting the mutuality of intimacy, he never comes to know who he really is, or develops his proper human potential. As long as he can evoke and manipulate an adoring audience, he feels great. When that manoeuvre ceases to be successful, there is a collapse into pathetic emptiness.

The roots of perversion are more complex. While it often manifests itself in atypical sexual behaviour, and can be understood in part as a failure to solve oedipal tensions, that is not the whole story. My understanding is that in this condition relationships are essentially about, not love, but the struggle for power, and that there is, at the centre, destructive anger and envy of a most primitive kind, which puts its origins right back into the early months of life.

I was interested by the comments of David Cantor in his recent book on serial killers. He remarks on how horrific it is that people can grow up in our society, for a time flourish, maybe marry and have a family, yet at a deep level be unaware that other people are truly human—the condition expressed legally as 'lack of concern' or 'lack of remorse'. However Cantor failed to link this with the killer's own experience as a dependent child—'a victim'—of also being treated as a thing—not truly human. The brutality of serial murder is an appalling example of 'doing as you were done by'.

Underlying much of what I have said is the basic human need for containment, for those boundaries which help us to feel safe. Hopefully we find it in our infancy, physically held and emotionally contained by our carers; and if we are fortunate enough to have that experience we internalise it, so that later we can do it for ourselves. We seek it later in the stability of the material world around us, in our network of relationships, in the social, political, religious structures and rituals of our adult lives. Often we have no notion of the extent to which we rely on these structures until they are no longer there. Much of the stress of moving house, changing jobs, is because the familiar, barely conscious points of reference vanish. I recall going on holiday to New England and finding so many familiar English names among the small communities there. I became conscious of how much those early settlers missed their native land, how frightened they were, and how brave and pathetic their attempts to feel more at home in that vast unknown land. I understood for the first time their need for a strongly fundamentalist religion to save them from going totally out of their minds.

We understand the narcissistic personality as the attempt of someone to provide for himself the containment which the care-givers failed to provide; while the perverse personality attempts to solve a similar problem by denying that there is any need for such containment and boundaries. There is no separation, no discernment or discrimination, like a child with a paint box who

119

puts many colours on his paper then swirls his brush around until it is all a muddy brown.

I sense a growing social awareness of the need for people to have the containment of structures and boundaries in order to feel secure enough to function adequately. Perhaps this is what John Major's ill-fated *Back to Basics* campaign was groping for, and some of Tony Blair's recent utterances seem to address the same issues. **

Perhaps the pendulum is beginning to swing in the other direction, in which case the greater danger may be that of replacing too-flexible social attitudes with various kinds of rigid fundamentalism. That I would not welcome—the damage to the individual is too high. Somehow we have to try and find a way of holding the tensions, of walking the tightrope. I encourage myself by the thought that the English have always been rather good at that sort of thing. After the religious wars of the seventeenth century, 'enthusiasm' became a dirty word. Since then, our notorious social apathy has served us in good stead and protected us from much of the political and religious extremes suffered by other societies!

Sexuality

And what of sex? What can I possibly say that is new about that over-exposed and under-valued aspect of human life? Under-valued because in recent times we have trivialised it—to our detriment. We have regarded it as an aspect of recreation, something to be played around with, sensually indulged in, picked up and dropped at our whim—as if it were a domestic pussy cat, when in fact we are riding a tiger!

Sex is about Life—about Life living us, rather than the other way round. I am moved by the way that a bereavement will often be followed by a burst of sexual activity, as if the brush of death calls forth an assertion of life. Sexual acting-out—an inappropriate affair, an adulterous relationship—is so often an attempt to ward off an incipient and sometimes deep depression. Even eccentric and bizarre sexual behaviour, examined closely, reveals a desperate attempt to hang on to something that feels real, when the personality is threatened by fragmentation or the annihilation of non-being.

I am not denying that sexual acting-out is often damaging. Nor am I denying that moral judgment is sometimes appropriate and necessary. But as a psychotherapist my task is one of understanding, and I speak from that vertex.

What I wish to say is that sexuality stems from the most primitive and profound depths of our being, and not to recognise that is to ask for trouble.

The Greeks talked of Dionysos, gave him an honoured place in their pantheon, and a period of celebration in their calendar, but they had no illusions about his power. He had to be given his due. Euripides' play *The Bacchae* is the story of a king, Pentheus, a good man if a bit narrow and self-righteous, who despises the annual celebrations and refuses to join in. At the end he is torn apart by the handmaidens of Dionysos, the Bacchae. Dionysos denied is ultimately more destructive than Dionysos accepted.

In our culture, we are not good at integrating this aspect of our being. Other countries have their festivities, the Mardi Gras, the Fasching, when normal restraints and boundaries are briefly set aside and no questions are asked. Catholic countries seem to manage it better than Protestant ones. I noted the comment by Cardinal Martini on his recent visit to Archbishop Carey. He said, ' In Italy we believe the ideal is set high so as to achieve something. In northern countries they think they must actually achieve the ideal, and they are anxious if they fail.' It is no coincidence that historically the English were seen as a melancholic nation, or the Nordic peoples full of gloom. I doubt it is just the climate!

In our contemporary society we are getting the worst of both worlds—the return of the repressed. Dionysos, long denied, is bursting out in all directions, in uncontrolled and unmanageable ways that are destructive because they are not sufficiently in the social consciousness. The answer is not the kind of sexual free-for-all which was fashionable, and did actually take place in certain circles, in the Sixties. The arrival of AIDS has anyway put that out of court. Nor is it in a return to some narrow and repressive morality which inhibits spontaneity, creativity and any real joy in living. Rather it is in making our peace with that aspect of our nature, holding it in our awareness, respecting it, giving it its due, and putting appropriate boundaries and constraints around it. In other words, in learning to ride the tiger.

Spirituality

What of religion, and our spiritual needs? While a few have the gift of mystical apprehension from a tender age, for most of us, spiritual experience and understanding is a late development.

Children think concretely. They will listen to stories as long as they are interesting, and are told by people they like. They have a capacity for magical thinking, but that is not the same as symbolic thinking—it is closer to the magician's tricks, and relates to their own unconscious phantasies and nightmares. As far as religious observance is concerned, my own feeling is that they should join in with the family pattern as long as they are willing, or can be induced with a modest degree of bribery. At the same time, I regard children going to Sunday School, or whatever, as in the same category as proper bed-times—a convenience for the parents which they positively need to preserve their own sanity and capacity to function. They should not feel guilty about that! As children approach puberty, they increasingly want to do other things on a Sunday rather than go to Church or Meeting, things involving their friends or their special interests, and this should be accommodated and respected as long as suitable arrangements can be made.

Adolescence brings a sense of the numinous alongside the upsurge of hormones. What also comes with adolescence is the capacity to think symbolically. We begin to appreciate poetry, as opposed to verse, and respond to music, not just rhythm and tune. We become concerned about social issues. We begin to address the wider, the ultimate questions about Life. It becomes possible to talk about the meaning of religion beyond the stories.

All this is a natural path of development as the young prepare themselves for their move into the adult world. Their spiritual growth is mostly intellectual, part of the curiosity about the world beyond 'home' going on alongside the rapid physical and emotional changes; but these developments are piecemeal, scattered, unintegrated. Which bits of the adolescent's potential will develop is often a matter of chance, of who they meet and what experiences they have at crucial points. Talking with someone sympathetic and stimulating can have lasting repercussions. At the same time, they react negatively to attempts to preach at them or coerce them into accepting someone else's schema for living.

As you may gather, I have doubts about direct attempts at religious education, though that may say more about my own personality than anything else! I have long believed that true religion is caught not taught. Expose them to it, yes; let them see that this is something important to you; let them hear you talking about it over the meal-table, living it out in whatever way is appropriate to you; but then accept that they have to find their own path up the spiritual mountain. I have long felt that we should perhaps treat religion as our grandparents treated sex—something to be hidden from the children as strictly for adults. That would guarantee their interest!

Commonly, religion begins to have real meaning when life brings us experience which shakes us to the core—the profoundly good experience of falling in love, the birth of a child; the tragedies that come close to all of us sooner or later—a death, unexpected illness, a car crash, the collapse of something that felt safe and solid. In the last two years, six of my contemporaries have had to face the death or impending death of an adult child. They, and those around them, find this profoundly shocking. It is out of sequence; it shouldn't happen like that. Security has gone. They will need to search for it elsewhere. In the end it may be a growth experience for them that they would not have had without the tragedy; but it is hard.

For most, spiritual growth is forced upon us in the middle years. Some small minority do indeed seem to be spiritually gifted in a quite atypical way and from a much younger age. In my experience they are often, though not always, people who have met up with suffering early, and beyond the norm. One of the most spiritually aware people in my own circle is someone whose earliest memories are as a two-year old being carried through her native city the night after the Allies had bombed it, and seeing the streets littered with dead bodies and scattered limbs. It is no surprise that she chose to work first with dying children, then became a social worker, and subsequently a psychotherapist. The ministry of healing was the only creative way forward for her.

Extreme experiences cause the normal boundaries to become attenuated. We live encapsulated within time and space, but sometimes we get a glimpse of the eternity beyond. Those glimpses may be rare but they are formative. They can change the pattern of our life. For people who are stressed beyond their capacity to bear, these glimpses may be more frequent and more powerful. This is why there is a link between religious insight and psychotic experience. Many religious leaders of the past, with their visions and wild utterances, would be lucky to avoid the schizophrenic label today. It is a fine line between those who can integrate this beyond-the-boundary experience, and those who cannot. Jung is a recent example of one who did, with great advantage. The Quaker, George Fox was another.

Perhaps this is why there tend to be many schizoid people in the Church—not just because religion is part of their intellectualist defence, though it most certainly can be, and not because they are just seeking out-of-this-world solace as their critics say, but because their suffering at the beginnings of life has made them more aware of the dimension of eternity. I would add that those with a marked schizoid dimension are potentially dangerous, since it is all too tempting to turn one's back on tasks that belong to being properly incarnate, and to rationalise that turning-away as a good thing. This is the Manichean heresy, and what a blight that has been on the life of the Church.

Psychodynamically this is a nice example of splitting—that mechanism we first use when very young of polarising good and bad, because to both love and hate one's parents is too painful and threatening to bear. The capacity to tolerate ambivalence is a maturational step, and not easily achieved. Even as adults, splitting into good and bad, black and white, is a defence we can readily fall into when threatened. The old Witch religion had as one of its beliefs that good and evil come inextricably mixed. That was a sound if uncomfortable doctrine. When life drives me to the point of screaming or despair, I recall Harry Williams' book *The True Resurrection*. In it he says, 'the Resurrection is a statement that God can make heaven out of a hell of a mess'. I find those words a great comfort.

Joining the Dance

I leave you with two quotations. One is well known. It is from the third chapter of the *Book of Ecclesiastes* and is one that I always find moving.:-

> 'To every thing there is a season, and a time to every purpose under heaven A time to be born and a time to die; a time to plant and a time to reap;
>
> A time to weep, and a time to laugh; a time to mourn, and a time to dance;
>
> He hath made everything beautiful in his time; also he hath set the world in their heart, so that no man can find out the work that God maketh from the beginning to the end.'

We live in time; it a fundamental of our incarnate existence. We each have a beginning and an end. Time structures our lives and gives them meaning, and we need to make our peace with it.

My second quotation is shorter—a mere phrase. Back in the 1960s Frank Lake wrote a contribution to a small book of essays entitled *We Must Love One Another or Die*. However you choose to interpret those many faceted words love and die, in that phrase there is profound truth, and it is that thought that I want to leave you with tonight.

I would also add my belief that human love, whether Eros, caritas or agape, is simply our incarnate manifestation of that creative spirit which brought the universe into being, and which is still creating it. It is our choice whether or not we join the dance.

---

* *The Anglican priest and psychiatrist, Dr. Frank Lake (1915-82), who founded the Clinical Theology Association, used L.S.D. as an aid to regression for a while in the 1950-60s. By the time I knew him, he had abandoned the drug since he felt he could achieve similar results without it. (Later, we came to reealise that L.S.D. was not without its dangers. A* *subsequent fashion for its recreational use resulted in a rash of drug-precipitated psychoses not dissimilar to what we have been seeing more recently from the abuse of cannabis.)*

Frank Lake's technique was impressive and convincing. He came to believe that a difficult birth experience was a major factor in the subsequent development of mental illness. His thinking is recorded in his book Tight Corners in Pastoral Counselling.

While I always felt that a difficult birth was only one of many factors influencing emotional development, nevertheless I became convinced of its significance as the first major transition of life, and the one which sets the pattern for all subsequent transitions. Much of the time what actually happened can only be inferred from a person's subsequent life history, but sometimes family myth confirms one's guess in quite a startling manner.

One has to remember that the experience of the baby and that of the mother are not necessarily the same. It is well known in medical practice that a very quick birth may be great for the mother but much too rapid for the infant, causing it physiological distres, since there is not enough time for the cranial bones to mould during the journey through the birth passage.

I also came to believe that the immediate post-partum experience of the neo-nate leaves its imprint—whether it is put into an incubator, left in isolation, moved into a separate nursery where its crying will not disturb the mother, or kept close to its mother's body.

The implications for obstetric care are immense!

More recently, Alessandra Piontelli's work on foetal experience published in her book From Foetus to Child *gives experimental evidence that these earliest experiences do indeed have subsequent significance.*

** Margaret Thatcher was the first woman to hold the role of Prime Minister in this country, and served between 1979 and 1990. She was a dominant personality who evoked powerful and mixed feelings in those around her. She undoubtedly changed the cultural climate of Great Britain during her years as head of government.

John Major was the Tory Prime Minister who succeeded her and held office from 1990 to 1997. His 'Back to Basics' campaign was an attempt to address some of the disturbing social issues of the day, including a high level of corruption in his party, but it was met with widespread derision.

His government was defeated by the Labour Party under the leadership of Tony Blair who went on to win two further General Elections.

(1994)

The Imprint of God

'The Universe is not only queerer than we
suppose, but queerer than we can suppose.'
J.B.S.Haldane

'God, who created all things in the beginning,
is himself created by all things in the end.
Olaf Stapledon

Today, as I address you, I feel somewhat nervous because
somewhere inside me, as an old friend, a contemporary, once said
to me, I am still wondering what I am going to do when I grow up.
I too laughed at that remark, but it contains a profound truth about
human beings, namely that in the depths of our personalities we
have no sense of the passing of time—what in the jargon of my
professional discipline we refer to as the timelessness of the
unconscious.

It is, of course, the stuff of my profession. An elderly woman of my
acquaintance still dresses in the style she has favoured since her
youth. One might unkindly call it tarty; it is certainly designed to
catch the eye, sexy and provocative. Yet the reality of her life is that
she has always been sexually frigid, and if any man made sexual
advances to her, he would be rebuffed in no uncertain manner. If
she had been of a younger generation she is the sort of woman who
would have cried rape and begun litigation at the drop of a hat.
She has only ever been interested in men who were rather gentle
and passive, and who have invariably been a disappointment to
her. Now that life is becoming more restricted for her with
increasing age, she cannot allow herself to take a taxi for fear that

128

she will be sexually attacked by the driver. It is all slightly ludicrous and deeply sad.

What this woman is acting out is something that happened to her when she was five years old when a man exposed himself to her, thus creating a great furore within the family. I suspect that behind that incident is the experience of an emotionally deprived little girl desperately seeking parental love but sending out inappropriate signals—if you like, a classic hysteric scenario. To witness that scenario being compulsively re-enacted many decades later is bizarre, and a glaring example of the timelessness of the unconscious.

Another patient, a counsellor in training has recently taken on some work in a medical setting. Her therapy with me is going well and we have, so I think, a good working alliance. However, she has taken on this work without having mentioned it to me, which fact takes me by surprise. It is uncharacteristic of her. Moreover, she clearly expects that I will disapprove both of her action and her secrecy about it. In reality I approve of her doing this work—she is ready for it and it is a good professional opportunity—and my reaction to her secrecy is one of curiosity. We explore the matter but it is a long time later before she comes to understand fully what she has been projecting on to me. I had become at that point her mother who could not let her daughter separate from her, and who resented and disapproved of any new initiative that took her daughter further from her. This is a major issue in the patient's therapy, and it was the first time it had emerged from beneath the cloak of compulsive compliance with which she relates to significant figures in her life. It is literally a matter of years before this patient comes to realise how frightened she has been of me/ her mother, and how this has interfered in her making full use of her therapy.

In the consulting-room psychotherapists make use of that timelessness of the unconscious as a routine part of our stock-in-trade. We rely on the fact that the crucial incidents and the primary relationships of our patients' lives are played out with us, the therapist. We call it the transference, and we learn to recognise it and manage it as part of our technique. Indeed it is there from the beginning, from the very first session with a patient, even from the very first telephone call or letter, if only we can recognise it (which of course we can't. It is only with hindsight that we can look back and see what was there—which is a very good reason for keeping full notes of those very first interactions even if you never make any further notes of any kind.) But of course those transference elements, that acting out of old relationships within the present are a part of ordinary life, of everyday encounters, and there is no way we can escape them. Our history is always with us and influencing our lives. The best we can hope for is to learn to recognise these transference elements and hopefully make our peace with them so that they do not unduly distort the present reality.

There is another kind of timelessness which operates throughout our social life, in any group activity, in the family, in organisations to which we belong, in the fields of politics, business, social change, war or religion. It is not strictly speaking timeless, but the time-scale is such that for all practical purposes it might as well be. I am referring to those kinds of behaviour which derive from in-built patterns inherited with our genes. In terms of evolution, biological evolution, human beings have not changed since the Pleistocene period, 15 - 40 thousand years ago. Our instinctual patterns are still those belonging to a hunter-gatherer animal living in small face-to-face groups, and with a sparse population density. We are by innate temperament protective of our own, suspicious of strangers, readily roused to aggression in defence of our kin and our territory.

For a time Homo Neanderthalensis and Homo Sapiens lived alongside each other with little to distinguish them, although there is no evidence that they interbred, and the child-rearing patterns differed. Current belief is that Neanderthal man left the care of the young to the females, while the males went off in their own separate group, while in Homo Sapiens both parents were involved with their offspring, hence the nuclear family as a unit. However, at some point there is a rapid change—the so-called Pleistocene Shift. While Homo Neanderthalensis had no burial ritual for his dead, after the shift we meet in Homo Sapiens recognisable burial practices and rituals such as the deposition of grave goods. At about the same time emerges primitive art—cave paintings; and with these two activities we must assume some capacity for symbolic thinking and the beginnings of religion. Not long after, in relative terms, Neanderthal Man disappears from the scene.

The inference then is that religious expression is an attribute peculiar to Homo Sapiens. Indeed, there has been a recent suggestion, to which I am inclined to subscribe, that we have a genetic endowment for religious experience. Neuropsychologists have even located an area in the brain, in the temporo-parietal region, which when electrically stimulated will give rise to religious experiences and feelings. (This also offers an explanation as to why people who suffer from temporal lobe epilepsy are often religiously gifted—Mohammed is an often-quoted example.)

We are no longer hunter-gatherers. In the days when we were, a balance existed between the individual, the social system and the environment. Then two things happened to disturb the balance. Firstly, an Ice Age developed, which increased the density of human population by squeezing large numbers of people into south-west Europe, the Middle East, and parts of Asia. At about the same time we took to farming, we developed technology which improved our living standards but also made us more destructive bringers of death. By successfully exploiting natural resources, our population grew, we had surpluses which allowed certain people to be freed from the daily drudgery of survival, we developed social hierarchies, lived in conurbations, became civilised—in a certain sense. We developed classes, castes, power elites, armies, empires, slaves and the exploitation of subject peoples. We began on a line of development which put us on a collision course with the social needs of the Palaeolithic hunter. 'What we call history ..... is merely the most recent catalogue of the products of that collision.' (Fox 1989)

But our genetic endowment has not changed. Nor is it likely to since we have interfered with those very biological processes which led to natural selection. We take steps to ensure that it is not just the fittest who survive. It is a mark of pride in being civilised that we care for the weak and helpless, have an elaborate system of medical care which has radically changed so-called natural processes, have eliminated so much disease which would have

131

culled the weak in times past, and feel frustrated that we don't achieve more than we already do. Social evolution has taken over where biological evolution left off.

But, but ..... in so many ways we have created a way of living that it is at odds with our innate tendencies, the timeless within us is at war with the times we have, and we feel the tension without knowing what it is that bothers us. The intense curiosity and impressive ingenuity of Homo Sapiens has solved so many problems of human life, and created so many others in the process. Perhaps this is the Good Lord's intention for us—another mode of evolutionary change—but it takes place on the back of our earlier programming which continues to drive with all the force of any instinctual endowment.

So, we have the timelessness of the individual unconscious, the timelessness of our unconscious as a species, our group unconscious if you like.

We also use the concept of timelessness to describe a different kind of experience. We speak of a timeless moment, an experience outside time, a moment of special significance which transcends the everyday and briefly puts us into contact with eternity. It is an experience that many people have, as Sir Alister Hardy discovered in his researches, but which for the most part we are reluctant to talk about. It can be triggered by a variety of sensory stimuli, a beautiful landscape, a sunset, a piece of music, an intense sexual experience. It is wordless but is felt to be of immense value; it can transform one's subsequent life; it is the basis of mysticism.

The psychotherapist in me suspects that at such time we are recovering a dim memory of life in the womb, of total at-oneness with the surrounding universe, of Eden before the expulsion from the Garden. It is one kind of explanation; it doesn't invalidate others. There are many levels of understanding, and they all have their place.

I liked the story told by Elaine Storkey in a recent (October, 1997) radio broadcast *Thought for the Day* about a small girl who had just acquired a baby brother. She was overheard, leaning over the baby's cot, saying, 'Hurry up and talk so you can tell me what it like being with God before you forget.' Out of the mouths of babes........!

Patterns

I am talking in various ways about patterns—about the innate patterns which shape our lives.

Much of my work as a psychotherapist is about recognising the patterns in the material my patients bring me, and in helping them to recognise them, understand their origins, modify, manage and live with them. Some can be changed—with difficulty. As Frank Lake used to say, 'Love + confrontation = pain + growth.' The pain can be enormous.

Some patterns cannot be changed, or so I have reluctantly come to believe. A computer analogy is useful. Our innate instinctual endowment is hardware, wired into the system and permanent. Those patterns we acquire after birth are like software, information fed to us out of experience, which can be modified—and that is what psychotherapy attempts to do, albeit slowly, clumsily and with difficulty.

But there is a class of software which has all the characteristics of hardware. This is the programming we acquire during roughly the first two years of life, while the brain is still developing, and the sutures in the skull have not yet closed. While memory as we normally think of it is located in the frontal lobes, our memories from this early period of our life seems to be stored in a more primitive part of the brain, the mid-brain. They are non-verbal, because pre-verbal, often more a matter of mood, of feeling, than of anything more structured. What is laid down is the presence or absence of a rhythm to life as mediated by the daily care of the small child. Is there a consistency of pattern to life—a regularity which the child can learn to recognise?—is there a constancy of the primary figure?—does the primary figure behave in a predictable way?—is the child handled physically a lot or a little?—is he in constant human company or left on his own for a long time? Is the world brought to him in such a way as to gradually make sense, or does it seem chaotic? These are experiences for which there are no words so they cannot be thought about in the way we ordinarily use that term, but they are enormously formative and condition the sort of person we become more than we know.

I have come to believe that it is almost impossible to produce change in this early software, so much so that I think that for all practical purposes it counts as hardware. A very intuitive therapist skilled at working at a pre-verbal level may be able to understand and interpret the moods that the patient brings and offer speculative reconstruction of how infancy was. (Bollas) However much understanding is gained, if the damage and deprivation from this early period is severe, it leaves a kind of vulnerability which one can hopefully learn to accept and manage, but one can never be as if that damage had not occurred.

These are the patterns of the individual's life experience, laid down upon a sub-stratum of innate, genetic patterning—some of it common to all human beings, some of it shared only with one's relatives.

We have, I believe, at long last got away from that hoary old nature/nurture debate about how we become who we are. The truth is that both are active. The current thinking is that hereditary accounts for about 60% of our characteristics, environmental influences about 40%. Whether you find that a source of reassurance and relief, or one of frustration and dismay depends, I guess, on where you are coming from. I have certainly had to shift my own perspective during my adult life. Before I had children, I used to believe that the difference between boys and girls was largely a matter of upbringing. My own young soon demolished that fantasy! And one of the joys of grandchildren is watching the developing resemblances to various other family members, the different combinations of characteristics, and the welding of all that with personal experience into a unique individual with his or her special potential.

Within the Clinical Theology Association we have long had a good-enough understanding of the patterning that goes to make individual development thanks to Frank Lake's particular gifts as a therapist and teacher. He grasped some fundamental principles of infant life and managed to condense them into a readily

134

transmissible format that could be understood by those of us with little or no specialised knowledge of the field. The course which he developed for the first-year seminars was brilliant in its way and provided a good and sound experience for the group participants at the time I was tutoring. I was never as happy with the second year syllabus when the course moved out into the wider world of social interaction .... and I gather that feeling is still around.

Evolutionary Psychology

In recent years, there has been some interesting new thinking in the realm of biology. One of the areas newly opening up is in that area I referred to a few minutes ago, namely that of our genetically innate behaviour patterns and their inappropriateness for our contemporary life. I think we now have a scientific basis for doing some radical re-thinking about out society and its problems. If we think of the human animal as innately a hunter-gatherer living in a very different world, we may have both more compassion for our short-comings and more hope for our ability to work out solutions.

The area of scientific study which is coming to be known as evolutionary psychiatry has some interesting and helpful things to say. In a way, Jung got there first with his concept of archetypes, which was his language for what I would call innate programming, and his intuitive insight has been backed by work in recent years from the ethologists, who study behavioural patterns in organisms living in their natural environment. This work, in turn, much influenced John Bowlby among others, and led him to develop the ideas of Attachment Theory. Although reviled at the time by the psychoanalysts, Attachment Theory is becoming increasingly accepted and influential, since it has the pragmatic sanction of illuminating observable clinical phenomena.

According to Anthony Stevens, the Jungian analyst, the concept of archetypal endowment is that with which each of us is born which prepares us for the natural life-cycle of our species in the natural world in which we evolved. A programmed series of stages, each mediated by a new set of archetypal imperatives, seeks fulfilment in the development of characteristic patterns of personality and behaviour. Each set of imperatives makes its own demands upon the environment. Mental health depends upon the provision of physical and social environments capable of meeting the archetypal needs of the developing individual. Should the environment fail to meet them, then the consequent frustration of archetypal intent may result in pathology. For example, we are programmed to learn to talk at a certain age, and we need the presence of other talking people from whom to learn. If we are deprived of that company for too long, we never do learn that basic skill. The cut-off age appears to be puberty, and there are records of unfortunate individuals reared in exceptional conditions who have suffered this experience, and who remain permanently mute.

Robin Fox deduces that the groups in which our species lived for 99.5 per cent of its existence consisted of about forty to fifty individuals, made up of approximately six to ten adult males, about twice that number of child-bearing females, and about twenty juveniles and infants. These were 'organic extended kinship groups' and they constitute what we might call 'the ancestral society' of our kind.

Such groups did not, of course, function in isolation. They came into frequent contact with other similar groups—hence the universal human rituals of greeting, visiting, feasting, making alliances, marriages, and wars.

These compact, intimate, extended kinship groups of forty to fifty members knew one another intimately and shared the same values, rules, customs, and mores, their beliefs being sustained by myth, ritual and religion. In all of them the family was the central institution, whether polygamous, monogamous, or polyandrous. When they got larger than this there was a natural tendency for groups to split and for one section of the community to move away to find another range. It is in order to live in such societies as this that nature has equipped us, and this fact is a crucial issue.

Anthony Stevens goes on to talk of '....the disruption of community-based kinship bonds as a result of migration, job mobility, experiments in town planning, and so on; the disruption of families through divorce or separation together with the rapidly increasing incidence of single-parent families; the loss of female support groups of the kind provided by traditional communities;

the lack of adequate provision for the secure and intimate care of children whose mothers go out to work; the occurrence of negative life events such as losing one's job, being passed over for promotion, mortgage rate increases, house repossessions, exam and interview failures, difficulty in acquiring the necessary skills demanded by employers, and sedentary work in artificial light and controlled atmospheres; the loss of myth, ritual and religion; the lack of contact with nature, the seasons and the primordial environment. All these factors are potentially productive of stress, insecurity and 'anomie' as well as skewed or distorted development. It seems likely that the various neuroses, psychopathies, drug dependencies, the occurrence of child and spouse abuse, to say nothing of the ever rising crime statistics, are not unconnected with Western society's inability to satisfy the archetypal needs of our kind.'

So where does all this leave us?

We have one world-wide overwhelming problem which keeps rearing its head in one place and another. It derives from the undoubted fact that we are innately territorial animals, and that we suffer as a species from over-population. Even if, in theory, we can feed the numbers of people on our planet, the main reason that we don't is not due to natural disaster but to war, and the social and political breakdown that war brings. Our innate aggression makes the density of population dangerous given our capacity for massive destruction.

How do we tackle it? Pol Pot found a kind of solution in Cambodia; Lenin and Stalin brought about the deaths of millions of their own countrymen; most people have forgotten that the Nazi party was 'Green' in its early days. These things will go on happening unless we find a better way.

So far, wide scale attempts to impose birth control have failed dismally, as in India, or have resulted in much personal suffering and distortion of the population balance, as in China. However, I listened recently to a broadcast talk by a man (a Muslim) who had run his community's contraceptive program for some twenty-five years, and who had eventually found that the only change which correlated with a drop in birth-rate was an expansion in the education of girls. He ruefully commented that if he had known that from the start, he would not only not have wasted vast sums of money, but he would have largely cracked the problem in his own country.

We are designed by our innate patterning to live in small face-to-face groups, and for some generations now the pressures have all been in the opposite direction. There have been undoubted benefits from this; a face-to-face society imposes many limitations upon its members. I personally was very grateful for the opportunity education gave me to move out of the small circle into which I was born. The danger is that too many people have lost a sense of belonging to a place or group, and lack the inner resources to compensate for that loss. In its place develops a pseudo self-sufficiency which readily descends into narcissism- a 'turning away from the life-giver' as the psychoanalyst Neville Symington calls it —which in turn breeds family breakdown and further narcissism. An escape into the quick-fix solutions to feeling good of random sex and drugs is just a few steps down the road.

The sad history of the American Indians and the Australian Aborigines over a very short period of time should remind us of what happens to vulnerable human groups when deprived of their territory and their established group living patterns.

Authority & the Church

Another response to the escape from the limitations of face-to-face group living is to deny that there are any limitations of any kind—that we can become whatever we choose to be—and an undermining of the proper authority which puts limits around unacceptable social behaviour.

The American psychoanalyst Charles Socarides in his book on the nature and treatment of sexual perversion says 'The high incidence of sexual abuse of children during the 1980s makes one conjecture that there may be a 'facultative' or 'epidemic form' of (non-clinical) paedophilia ..... Such epidemic or facultative forms of sexual perverse pathology have been known to occur at times of social disequilibrium, when there is no 'authoritative prohibition by society' (Freud) against sexual license. In a sense they represent the enactment of an earlier historical belief in the adulation and primacy of instinctual discharge processes, rather than a belief in the value of the sexual object per se.'

The phrases I want to highlight are 'times of social disequilibrium' and 'no authoritative prohibition by society'. The first is a matter of observation; the second leads one to think about the role of the Church in these times. It is difficult in our so-called liberal times for the Church to be authoritative without being accused of authoritarianism, but that last phrase of Socarides—a belief in the value of the sexual object per se—is a sentiment at the heart of Christian values, and would seem to me to be a good base from which to build. The argument against perversion is that it exploits the object, the other, and demeans that other by treating him or her as less than fully human, as a thing.

What are the implications for the Church in these ideas? I hesitate. I have powerful inhibitions against commenting on an institution that has survived so much for so long, that serves so many functions at so many different levels, that has all kinds of subtleties that both keep it on track and also mitigate against change. In some ways I am tempted to feel that it is currently suffering from too much change, or too many attempts to change it. If in some ways it seems at a low ebb today, it has known far worse periods such as in the eighteenth century. I have a feeling it may be poised for a latter-day equivalent of the nineteenth century Evangelical Revival, though not, I hope, in quite that form!

Whatever! In our contemporary scientific era it must make its peace, its rapprochement, with those ideas that are the everyday currency of thinking people, and some of the ideas I am touching upon tonight have their relevance.

If we accept the notion that Man is at depth still the hunter-gatherer of the Pleistocene period, it has certain implications. I believe, and you may think it so self-evident to be hardly worth mentioning, that the church group works best when it is a face-to-face group, living and working in a certain limited area, sharing common problems and situations and hence understanding each other's lives. (As I say this I am also aware that small communities can become mad as can large ones.) I imagine that in the urban and suburban areas where so many of us live nowadays, there have to be other ways of creating a sense of shared community, a shared project or purpose around which a group can unite. I like the idea of churches reverting to their mediaeval pattern of use as the local meeting place, function hall, theatre, market. Come to think of it, my own bit of the Church, the Society of Friends, manages this without thinking about it, and without detracting from the central mystery of the Meeting for Worship.

I recently heard John Bell of the Iona Community arguing cogently for the use of vernacular furniture and furnishings, where there is a local tradition to be drawn upon, to emphasise the sense of particularity of the group. In his Highland setting he favoured Orkney chairs and hand-loomed tweeds, and I could see the attraction! In his words, anything better than the drab, limp blue bit of cloth he meets everywhere he goes which gives no sense of place or significance.

I am speaking of the Church as meeting us at the small social group level of living, and I think it has taken this on board for the most part though actualising it is another matter! I wonder if women priests have a particular ministry in this area. Historically, it is the women who hold the small group together while the men are away hunting, or about those hunting-equivalents—business and war. Contemporary young women, and men, may wish to reject the stereotype of the hearth-centred gossiping domestic female, but her social skills are invaluable, not to say vital, in basic terms. Once we realise what they are for, we may be able to make use of them in a wider context, and with due respect.

I find myself wondering at this point about the flirtation with paganism, with the remnants of Celtic ritual, that is currently fashionable both inside and outside the Church. Is it perhaps an attempt to make contact with a time when we were more in touch with our basic nature, when our pattern of life was closer to that of our Pleistocene ancestors? I can sympathise with the motive, though truth to tell, the human race was embarked on its collision course of history long before our Celtic forebears were rampaging through Europe with their magical steel Excalibur swords.

140

Attachment & Status

Scientific evidence points to the existence of two groups of innate patterning, two great archetypal systems, one concerned with attachment, affiliation, care-giving, care-receiving, and altruism, the other concerned with rank, status, discipline, law and order, territory and possessions. These may well be the basic patterns on which social adjustment and maladjustment, psychiatric health and sickness depend. Both can function healthily when evoked in appropriate circumstances, but either can give rise to pathology when their goals are frustrated or when they are inappropriately activated. In their book *Evolutionary Psychiatry* Anthony Stevens and psychiatrist John Price argue, and persuasively so, that psychiatric disorders are manifestations of ancient adaptive strategies that are no longer necessarily appropriate but can only be adequately understood, and therefore treated, by seeing them in terms of the development of the human race, not just the development of the individual person.

For example, that widespread affliction of the human spirit, depression, is frequently precipitated by loss, typically the loss of a significant figure. However, Stevens and Price argue that it can also be an adaptive response to losing rank and conceiving oneself as a loser. In circumstances of defeat and enforced subordination, an internal inhibitory process comes into operation which causes the individual to cease competing and reduce his level of aspiration. This inhibitory process is involuntary and results in the loss of energy, depressed mood, sleep disturbance, poor appetite, retarded movements and loss of confidence characteristic of depression

The adaptive function of the depressive response is to facilitate losing, and to promote accommodation to the fact that one has lost and must accept the subordinate role and the loss of resources that this brings. It thus prevents the loser in a status conflict from suffering further injury and possibly death. At the same time, it preserves the stability and competitive efficiency of the group by minimising intra-group conflict. One might see depression in these terms as a yielding sub-routine of a ritual conflict, and its opposite, mania, as a winning sub-routine, the object of the yielding sub-routine being damage limitation, that of the winning sub-routine

141

status preservation. Both sub-routines ensure that social change is accomplished relatively quickly without too much disruption of group activities, and that once it has occurred it will prove lasting.

One can see that in the primitive hunter-gatherer group, these behaviour patterns facilitated the survival of the group, and the depression of the individual member was in the service of the group. Clinical depression as we know it can thus be seen as a pathological aberration derived from this adaptive emotional mechanism. Why some people have a particularly low threshold for the triggering of the depressive response is a complex issue involving genetics, family history, early attachment experience, stressful life events etc. However, there does seem to be a growing consensus that a critical factor influencing vulnerability concerns the issues of rank assessment, and consequent levels of self-esteem. Addressing these can be a significant focus of therapy.

If depression can be understood in terms of the dynamics of the hunter-gatherer group, so too can those spacing disorders which include the schizoid, paranoid and schizophrenic disorders. Stevens and Price argue that in the primitive group, these personality types can provide the kind of charismatic leadership which a group needs when the time comes to split off from the too-large parent group, and go off to pastures new. They have a shamanic quality necessary for a new leader to bring about the split; they can also be very dangerous and bring disaster in their wake as we know to our cost from contemporary history. Also, sadly for the individual, we seem to produce more of these personalities than we can find use for in our contemporary society.

I have given you but two short examples of how an evolutionary perspective can add to our understanding of psychopathology. It does not replace the understanding we already have in terms of individual development and internal psychodynamics, but it does add a dimension and in so doing sheds light into some still dark corners. I hope that in time, when we have assimilated these ideas, they will help us in our task of pastoral care and compassion.

The Church, I believe, has a good understanding of the one basic archetypal system—that relating to attachment, care-giving and – receiving, and altruism. It may fall down when it comes to putting it into practice, but its values reflect that innate basic patterning. It is much less comfortable with the other great system that I have touched on—that relating to status, law and order, territory and possessions—which reflects our phylogenetic history of living in small hunter-gatherer groups. The Church has tended to adopt a negative, repressive, disapproving stance in this direction while at the same time the institutional organisation is riddled with these issues—a nice case of the return of the repressed, as we therapists would say. I would like to see it facing this group of issues more honestly, to re-think its position in order to contribute more creatively to the wider social debate, and to minister more effectively to the suffering individual.

The Need for Meaning

On a different level of meaning, one of our basic human needs is to live in a world that makes sense and has significance. This is something that the good-enough mother gives to her child in the early weeks and months of its life by the continuity and consistency of her daily care. She does it without thinking about what she does, and the infant learns to recognise the patterns without knowing that it does. Human beings are very good at recognising patterns—they do it far better than any machine. If the mother is hopelessly chaotic and inconsistent, there is a real danger that the child will become mad, or inconsequential and a danger to itself.

What the mother does for the child, social institutions do for the human group. They present to their members a way of experiencing and understanding the world. In Stevens' words, 'All societies codify themselves; and their innate continuity depends upon the ability of new members to assimilate the code. Were this not so, the alternative would be anarchy and a collective incapacity for competition or defence. Because of its fundamental importance for the survival of any human community, the moral code has everywhere been accorded the dignity of divine sanction.' He goes on to say that, '... it seems highly probable that a propensity to religious forms of symbolism and belief exists as an innate potentiality in human nature.'

I believe one of the many functions of religion is to present its believers with a Weltanschauung, a perspective which enables them to make sense of the world they live in and their life experiences. It almost doesn't matter what that sense is as long as it is internally consistent, and also consistent with culturally perceived reality. Any story is better than nothingness. Christianity offers a way of viewing the human condition which has been very powerful and very attractive at certain times in history and to particular peoples. We must suppose that it has been so because it has resonated with their needs and hopes—it has encapsulated some basic truths. If the Church is currently flourishing less well in our society than elsewhere or at other times, we need to ask why. One reason must be the development of the scientific Weltanschauung as an alternative and antagonistic world-view. Maybe it was inevitable that they should be seen as in opposition— part of our primitive thought patterns is to see things in terms of black or white, right or wrong, a characteristic if you like of the paranoid-schizoid phase of infant development, although it is interesting that Erasmus Darwin, the grandfather of Charles who anticipated many of Charles's ideas, was quite clear in his mind that it was the hand of God that fuelled the evolutionary process. It is time we got beyond our primitive splitting thought-processes to acknowledge the underlying unity of all things, that the patterns underpinning the material universe and the innate patterns which make us what we are, are all of a piece.

I don't know whether any of you have come across fractal geometry. It made quite a stir in the scientific press a few years ago but I believe is now generally accepted and no longer controversial. I am not a mathematician but I was by chance privileged to hear a talk by Benoit Mandelbrot on his formulations. He had discovered that the mathematics underlying natural living forms is quite different from the kind of geometry we were taught at school; that very complex shapes can be expressed in surprisingly simple equations once you know how. I have since seen many pictures of these equations mapped out on to paper—the pictures are curiously beautiful; they remind me of the tortuous shape of a piece of coral, or a fragment of a complex Paisley pattern, or the map of a very rugged bit of coastline. What is also odd is that if a

144

portion of the pattern is magnified, the enlarged portion exhibits just as much complexity as the original piece, and that one can continue that process ad infinitum. It is as if a quite simple bit of information or patterning underlies an immense complexity of form. Listening to Benoit Mandelbrot, and I had gone with some reluctance to hear him, I experienced one of those curious timeless moments as if I had glimpsed an eternal truth. (I only recently realised that Leibniz had expressed the same idea before as early as 1714, in his *Monadology*, when he suggested that our universe had been selected from an infinity of possible universes so that a minimum of laws would lead to a maximum diversity of results.)

A New Theology

Another interesting bit of scientific thinking has come recently from the biological sciences, in the theory of complexity, as put forward by Stuart Kauffman and his associates at the Santa Fe Institute. They argue that once living things reach a certain size, they become self-organising. They somehow develop the capacity to become ever more complex, and that this self-organising tendency towards ever-increasing complexity operates throughout the natural world. The Santa Fe group understand evolution not simply as the result of natural selection, but as a marriage between natural selection and spontaneous order.

While much of Kauffman's thinking is highly technical and mathematical, some at least of his book *At Home in the Universe* is eminently readable and a real joy. I liked this passage because it mirrors my own observation.

'If the universe is running down because of the second law (of thermodynamics), the easy evidence out of my window is sparse—some litter here and there, and the heat given off by me, a homeotherm, scrambling the molecules of air. It is not entropy but the extraordinary surge towards order that strikes me. Trees grabbing sunlight from a star eight light-minutes away, swirling its photons together with mere water and carbon dioxide to cook up sugars and fancier carbohydrates; legumes sucking nitrogen from bacteria clinging to their roots to create proteins. I eagerly breathe the waste product of this photosynthesis, oxygen ... and give off the carbon dioxide that feeds the trees. The biosphere around us sustains us, is created by us, grafts the energy flux from the sun into the great web of biochemical, biological, geological, economic and political exchanges that envelopes the world. Thermodynamic be damned. Genesis, thank whatever lord may be, has occurred. We all thrive.'

I finds something curiously exciting about these ideas, of an inherently simple piece of information, or a simple living cell, producing an infinite complexity of form. I am reminded of the those words at the beginning of St. John's Gospel, 'In the beginning was the Word...' and a shiver goes down my spine. How did St. John know? How do the mystics know? How do they somehow manage to transcend time and touch eternity?

I think that much of the doctrine and the rituals of the Church embody or resonate with the basic patterns of human existence, and it would be interesting to look in some detail at them with that understanding. That is why the Church has survived. If it can get back to that basic understanding—if individuals within the Church can talk with that understanding—it will be relevant and be seen to be relevant. In mediating between basic human patterning and the demands laid upon us by the particular times and circumstances of our contemporary lives, it will continue to play its part in the different kind of evolution that is the task before the human race.

And in that task we need Hope. Rather, I would say that hope or a basic optimism is a normal attribute of living things in health. But we all have times when life is tough, we have reverses, there is always death and disaster to contend with, it is easy to feel discouraged and become sick. At these times we need a Faith by whatever name to make life worth the struggle.

For many of us, scientific rationalism and materialism has failed. In our society, despair, often masked by a kind of manic over-compensation, is all too prevalent, and drug-taking, sexual promiscuity, compulsive shopping and such-like acting-out does not lead to any lasting satisfaction. Narcissism is rampant. The Church as the Guardian of Hope is desperately needed, but it has to be a Hope that has some meaning for human beings reared in a scientific way of thinking, that is consonant with that mode of thinking not opposed to it, that does not insult our intelligence and credulity. I do not think that an impossibility. Indeed, I think it is easier now than it has ever been.

The greatest danger to the Church is now, as always in my view, in the Manichaean heresy—a repudiation of the incarnate world in favour of a disembodied spirituality. I can understand the temptation; I have my own schizoid bits, and when the going gets rough the urge to retreat to the metaphorical monastery can be powerful. (I say metaphorical monasteries because real monasteries are very well-grounded places in my limited experience!) One can understand that in past times when life was harsher and more brutal than ours is today, it would have seemed like the only sane and sensible option. I don't think it works. If Geoffrey Moorhouse' fantasy *Sundancing* is anywhere near the truth, the dream that created the community of Skellig Michael ended in a nightmare.

Where is God in all this? I am, I suppose, preaching an incarnational theology, seeing God at work in the world—a world which is his creation. I like Lionel Blue's words in his autobiography *A Backdoor to Heaven*, ' ... I understood that reality does not have to evaporate in order to become religious. I did not need to spiritualise things away, I had only to sanctify and hallow what already existed.'

I have always liked the Hindu concept of the world as God at play, God disguising himself so thoroughly in so many ways that He himself forgets who He is. That is not to deny the Transcendental God, the High God whom the Hindus call Brahma, who is essentially unknowable, but I am always on the alert against that schizoid splitting which has so bedevilled Christianity and set God at odds with His creation.

I don't find this position always easy. I cannot but feel that the crocodile was a mistake—that God got out of bed on the wrong side that day; and I feel much the same about the slugs which inhabit my garden! And where was God in the killing fields of Pol Pot, in Nazi Germany and Stalin's Russia? And where is He today in Ruanda and Bosnia? Intellectually, I know, the answer is 'suffering'. The reality is well-nigh unbearable, and unthinkable.

The Destruction of Thinking

It often seems that the ones who suffered most have least to say. The men who survived the Japanese internment camps were rarely willing to talk about what happened to them although their families were grimly aware of the changes in them.

We see a similar reaction to the victims of rape, of incest, of child abuse—they are so often silent. They cannot talk, they cannot think about their experience, they can only feel. They have no words. As psychotherapists, our work is first to enable them to feel their feelings, then to help them find words to describe what happened. It is only much much later that they can begin to think about the unthinkable.

The destruction of thinking, in another, in oneself, is a disturbing phenomenon and one that any psychotherapist meets in due course.

One of the things I have found hard to recognise is the way madness destroys the capacity to think. Psychotic process can be very subtle in its manifestations. You can think you are dealing with a ordinary, rational human being, conversation appears to be developing well, when at some point he/she makes a wild statement, asserts that something is what it patently isn't, denies the reality of something that is under his/her nose; and no attempt to help him face it gets you anywhere. You begin to wonder who is mad around here. Have you got it all wrong? Perhaps the other's perspective is the real one. You feel disoriented. You can't think clearly, a paralysis takes over.

With practice and a good supervisor, one learns to recognise this for what it is and rescue oneself from it, although it remains a curiously disturbing experience. It leaves me wondering uncomfortably what it must be like when one is caught in a social situation which is becoming mad. Perhaps that same paralysis of thought overtook some of those caught up in Nazi Germany when outsiders recognised that something was going seriously wrong. And how did people survive the long, paranoid madness that was Stalin's Russia? The faces of Russian dignitaries photographed at that period seem to me to belong to men who have looked upon the Gorgon's face and been turned to stone, men who dared not feel or think. Is it any wonder that we now have so much crime, delinquency and despair in the new Russia.

I wonder, too, about some of the things in our society that we dare not think about or pretend not to see. While the value we place on individual liberty and personal fulfilment has brought much that is positive, not least to women, I feel we are as yet unwilling to acknowledge the price we have paid in terms of social morality, family breakdown, the failure to nurture our children in an optimal fashion, and the long-term consequences we have set in train.

Where is God in the middle of all this? The Christian answer can only be—on the Cross. That central doctrine of Crucifixion and Resurrection embodies a deep truth about us and the created universe in which we live. It is a unique contribution to human insight. It is something that gets played out at all levels of existence. It is not a comfortable doctrine. We can all at times echo those words of desperation, 'My God, my God, why has thou forsaken me?'

How to think about God in a scientific age. I have offered an image that may seem very abstract and intellectual. It doesn't feel so to me; I find it profoundly moving and immediate, and oddly comforting. I must admit also to thinking about God at times in ways I would have been ashamed to own when younger—as a large safe figure holding my hand and keeping me safe, as a shoulder to weep on, as a parent against whom to rage and protest when life is manifestly unfair, as a power to mobilise my adult capacities when my miserable child or tiresome adolescent is in the ascendant. These images are all inadequate, they are all hopelessly simplistic, they all have a grain of truth in them. They say more about me than about God and yet ... when I summon them to mind, something changes; and I no longer despise them because the Ultimate Reality is, and always will be, beyond our comprehension.

Some time in the Sixties Frank Lake gave a talk on the then Third Programme entitled, as I recall, *The Many Faces of God*. His theme, less startling perhaps now than then, was that our image of God is very much influenced by what we project of our own internal

149

parents. He went on to describe how the different personality types each had their own characteristic distortions of the God image—the depressive's severe superego creating a judgmental and disapproving God for whom one was never good enough; the schizoid creating a God far outside and beyond His Creation who encouraged one to retreat from the real world into a pietistic spirituality; and so on. It was an insight I found extremely valuable.

I have come to accept that we do all make our personal projections on to the image of God, and that it is inevitable that we do so. It is just a part of being human, and nothing to be ashamed of. However, I believe we do have a duty to try and understand what it is we are projecting and to gradually withdraw those elements; that is part of our own personal and spiritual growth. It is a lifetime's task, and it is never complete. That does not matter in itself; what does matter is the journey. Equally it follows that we all will have a different concept of God. I don't think that that matters either as long as we can use those differences to expand our understanding.

What is deadly is when we come to believe that we alone have the definitive understanding—that is the sin of spiritual pride!

You will have realised by now that I do not personally believe that there is any innate contradiction between religion and science, although I accept that there are all sorts of discrepancies that need to be integrated. I have as my base a belief that Truth is a unity, that indeed the whole of Creation is a unity. If we cannot always see that, that is our problem. I note that nowadays, in academic life, it tends to be the faculties of Arts and Humanities who contain the majority of religious unbelievers, those of Engineering and Science those who have found some kind of faith—with, of course, some notable and vociferous exceptions!

There seems to be a growing consensus that the two fields address questions of quite different orders, the one deals in matters that in theory are capable of proof, the other where we never can have proof in the scientific sense. What is also interesting is that there are questions that arise in the scientific domain that can only have religious answers, such as 'What is the purpose of life?'; and vice versa, there are questions that arise in the religious domain that demand a scientific answer. In a sense, the area I am speaking to this evening comes into this latter category.

I have endeavoured to present to you some new ideas with which to think about innate human patterning. They are not really so new of course. At the beginning of this century C.G.Jung was to talk about archetypes and archetypal behaviour; a different language but the same phenomena. And I suspect if one went back in the history of the old nature-nurture debate one would find others struggling to describe what they had dimly perceived, but which for so long has been unfashionable to admit to. Like all basic truths they come around again and again but always with a subtly different, a contemporary, slant. What is interesting about the current version is that it has come from the scientists, the biologists and archaeologists, who can back up their speculations with hard evidence.

What I have been trying to offer in my discursive remarks is a biological framework within which to think creatively about many puzzling social phenomena. I am not suggesting that the past was idyllic, either a few hundred years ago before our Industrial Revolution brought unprecedented change, or many thousand years ago when we were still hunter-gatherers. I am making a plea that we take on board the new scientific insights about human nature, seeing the natural law as a part of God's creation, to be respected as such. I am also, by inference, asserting my belief that the schizoid position, the Manichean heresy, however seductive, is ultimately blasphemous and a blight on the Church.

I think that our society badly needs what the Church has to offer, but that the apparent opposition of the religious world-view and the scientific world-view too often interferes with the Church's message being heard. That opposition is false and with more recent scientific insights, no longer tenable, but the Church has work to do in integrating these new insights into its own thinking.

I believe that religion is still the bastion of morality in the sense that without divine sanction, morality gradually but inexorably decays. Liberalism, humanism, is not enough (and I say that with regret.) One can interpret 'divine sanction' in a wide sense, which is what I have tried to do by in effect saying, this is the way God made the world and we had better respect it or we are in deep trouble.

And respecting it means seeing the world as it is, not how we would like it to be or according to some ideological schema. If we see only our own clan as human, and the Jews or the Communists or the Croatians or the Ulster Catholics (or Protestants) as sub-human, then we are creating desperate problems for ourselves. However, at the same time we do need to recognise that deep-seated innate part of us which clings to our own and is suspicious of strangers and those who are different. We might do better to accept that reality and order our affairs accordingly.

We are equally laying up problems for ourselves if we pretend that men and women are really the same apart from superficial appearance; or that children can be brought up just as well by people who do not love them as by people who do.

As human beings we are all involved in that incredible evolutionary development of our species going only God knows where. Human evolution is no longer a purely biological matter—it has not been so for a very long time. It long ago became a matter of using our intellectual and emotional capacities to work with our basic biology; and *with* is the operative word here. The struggle for basic survival has been replaced by another, different but equally taxing struggle. Such is the time-scale that even the greatest amongst us can make only a tiny contribution; but even the least amongst does make a contribution, for good or ill.

We all have our pennyworth to contribute—and this is mine for now!

(1998)

Epilogue

*

Retirement

I never expected to retire—not retire as in give up work altogether. Rather I imagined myself just gently fading away, rather like the Cheshire Cat in *Alice*, until only the smile remained. Life without psychotherapy was unimaginable.

After all, I had discovered a vocation as a toddler as I tried to make sense of the emotional tensions between the adults of my child's world. (I am not claiming anything unique in this—I suspect most of my colleagues acquired their vocation at a similar age as they struggled to empathise with their mothers.) That vocation acquired a particular shape in my teens when my interminable reading led me to the shelves of psychoanalytic literature in our excellent municipal library. I was hooked! I was totally fascinated by this curious and utterly different perspective on the world which opened up to me. It gave me permission to think for myself about all sorts of issues which were concerning me, and a framework other than the unsatisfactory (to me) mores on offer at home and school. It represented intellectual freedom, and the promise of living my own life, not other people's idea of what that life should be. Subversive stuff indeed!

I read and read and read, and if I only understood a fraction of what I was reading, it didn't matter. I was confident that one day I would, and in the meantime it gave me more than enough to be getting on with.

Psychodynamic psychology, Freudian variety, became one of the twin foci of my life, the other being my close personal relationships; and so it has remained for fifty years and more. It has taken a lot of juggling, too, since in reality each of those foci was a lifetime's job in itself had I but known it, but I could never feel that one made much sense without the other however difficult it was to keep both balls in the air.

So where am I now, having hit seventy-two last summer. You could say that I am indeed doing my Cheshire Cat act. I have one or two patients not quite ready to let me go; one or two old ones returning for help with a current crisis; one or two who contact me from time to time just to make sure I am still alive in case they ever need me again! I am happy with this arrangement. I enjoy the contacts. I am still interested in them and their lives. I still feel I have something to offer without the stress of the full-scale involvements of yesteryear.

It has happened rather sooner than I had expected because of the demands of that other part of my life, but too soon to retire at seventy-odd? Surely not!

So why am I not entirely content with where I am at? The truth is that there has been a sea-change. My life-long obsession is no longer an obsession—and I miss it!

I can say a number of thing about this new state of mind. At some level I know that I have found out what I needed to know, and that I have done what I needed to do, and that is a relief, but also strange. It is as if I am just about ready to begin living at the point at which I shall have to depart—but I think that is a not uncommon feeling, and is saying something about the timelessness of the unconscious.

I have to confess, too, to a certain disillusion with psychotherapy and what it can and cannot achieve, as compared with the unrealistic optimism of my youth. I have learned that damage that is very early cannot be wholly undone, particularly if it gets into the psychosomatic domain. (To use IT jargon, it behaves like hardware not software.) The pain can be ameliorated, the distorted reactions managed, one can learn to accept and forgive one's

157

history, but one's history it remains. It can be lived with, but not wiped out.

I have learned that while we can help people understand their past, and can help them re-interpret it, we cannot reinstate it. How many cf my patients have wished that they could have had therapy earlier in life, before they reared their own children and made so many unnecessary mistakes, and passed their own suffering on to the next generation. How often has a patient, after a lengthy and painful struggle, reached the point where he/she feels able to commit to an intimate relationship, only to find that they have let slip potentially rewarding opportunities, or that it really is too late to begin rearing a family. Yes, we all have that kind of mourning to do, and when we have done it life can open up in the most unlikely ways, and it is that knowledge and that hope which we therapists have to hold in mind as we watch the struggles; but the loss is real. Time is a one-way stream.

I have learned too that those innate qualities of temperament which made it relatively easy for me to acquire a therapeutic stance —the capacity for empathy, the willingness to enter another's world, a certain patience and ability to wait, to tolerate not-knowing, to give the other lebensraum and time—these qualities have been less than helpful in dealing with a parent's slowly developing senile dementia, or with the dyslexia which runs like a thread through my family. The first went unrecognised for far too long. The second was universally unrecognised in its full implications until very recently. (It is not just difficulties in reading and writing, it is an atypical form of brain organisation and its various manifestations include difficulties in sequencing, and problems of memory. It has its compensations too. The dyslexics of my acquaintance are all great talkers, with a considerable capacity for creative thought and exceptional spatial ability They also manifest, most of the time, a robust idiotic optimism!) Both conditions are essentially hardware problems (confirmed by brain scans) and need a much more hard-edged reality-oriented management than sits comfortably with the psychotherapeutic mode which is my norm.

As when dealing with the small minority of deeply destructive patients, I have had to learn that what is normally creative and facilitating, in certain situations can be an inadequate response; and that has been a hard lesson to learn.

What I have found equally difficult is the recognition that therapy, even extensive and highly-skilled therapy, does not necessarily make us compassionate, honourable or mature in our interactions. While I have experienced great kindliness and warmth from many of my fellow professionals, I have also witnessed as much ruthless self-assertion, destructiveness and naked power battles as would disgrace an industrial boardroom. It would seem that psychoanalysis alone is not enough.

I have come to suspect that psychotherapeutic understanding is rather like religion—essentially caught rather than taught. That is not to deny the value of good teaching or of a well-planned course of study. Rather, that if not offered with sensitivity, these can interfere as much as help, can result in closed minds rather than open ones, rigid stances rather than creative curiosity. I think too, that as with religion, each generation has to discover it for itself in its living truth. Attitudes and expectations change, language changes, what is meaningful for one generation may strike no chords for the next. The deep underlying truths, the nature of the human condition, they do not alter; but the way we perceive them, the way we formulate them, that is always changing. The first time I recommended to someone a book that had been seminal for me, only to learn that it was now out of print, I felt shocked. Now I may feel sad but I do not worry. The truth remains—to be found again, or articulated in another way. Better that than the psychotherapeutic equivalent of 'ancient verities chanted by uncomprehending small boys in archaic languages'—(a friend's comment on his religious culture!)

So—my attention is drifting away to other matters of interest that have been sitting on hold for far too many years. Perhaps they are not really so different. I am increasingly aware of the unconscious forces at work in the wider world of politics and international affairs, and fascinated by those long-term shifts in culture which take place over decades, if not lifetimes, and so are difficult to comprehend and conceptualise.

I am still obsessed by origins, by how people come to be the way they are, but it is the origin of the human race, and of my Celtic and Viking forebears in particular, that increasingly occupies my reading time. The empathic attempt to enter others' inner worlds is even more difficult and tantalising than in the consulting room, but equally fascinating. There is more of archaeology and history and literature to be explored than I shall ever have time for, so I had better get on with it while I can. I have had my fill of the heat of battle, but I am glad that there are others to take on the challenges.

My chief regret now is that the psychodynamic understanding which is the basis of our work has not yet become more widely integrated into the common intellectual life of our culture. There are so many areas which would benefit from it, which do not make any sense without it; but as a society we are very resistant to such insights, and so we waste our resources and we waste the only true wealth—our people.

However, I do see signs of hope. The increasing numbers of trained therapists may make work harder to come by, but it is forcing us out into the marketplace, and making us think more about communicating the psychodynamic culture. (It is hard to recall that when I began my professional life in a psychoanalytic desert, my chief problem was in keeping my head above water and not getting totally overwhelmed by the sheer volume of work!) The current situation may be tough in terms of earning a living but it does leave us more time to think, and particularly to think about wider social issues in psychodynamic terms.

Hannah Segal has set a courageous example in her writings over the years. Opus has provided a valuable forum for discussion.

There is the occasional radio programme nowadays in which psychoanalysis is discussed seriously and with respect (although it appals me how many intellectuals who should know better seem to think that it all began and ended with Freud!)

In our immediate locality there are several enterprises applying a psychodynmic perspective to wider issues, and the London scene seems to be buzzing with analytic ferment.

Perhaps most importantly, our perspective on infant and child development has received much confirmation from work done in other disciplines—from long-term developmental studies, from neuro-science, from ethology—whose conclusions are research-based and far from speculative. If some of this work suggests that we may need to modify our professional time-frame in places, and clarify some of our ideas of what is normal and what pathological, nonetheless I believe it brings our discipline into the scientific mainstream, and that can only be of huge benefit.

The struggle for psychodynamic understanding has been and still is a fascinating enterprise, and for me personally it has been a compulsively intriguing, if sometimes painful, journey.

I would not willingly have missed it.

(2003)

End-note

'Sorrow may be fated, but to survive and grow is an achievement all its own.'

R.Coles. *Children of Crisis.*

'... never forget that your clients, your patients, have bodies as well as minds, and that the symptoms and problems for which they consult you are reflections, derivatives, and manifestations of the great human problems implicit in whatever stage of the life-cycle they are in.

... never forget that your clients exist within society—a society of which they are both beneficiaries and victims, of which they are both protected members and casualties.

... Winnicott has famously said that 'there is no such thing as a baby', meaning that babies make no sense without a mother. Similarly, there is no such thing as a mind without a body, and there is no such thing as a person without society. We are all members of one another.'

Charles Rycroft. 'The last word'
(*British Journal of Psychotherapy 11.3, 1995*)

'Believe nothing, no matter where you read it, or who said it—even if I have said it—unless it agrees with your own reason and your own common sense.'

The Buddha
563-483 BC.

Appendix:
The Clinical Experience

The previous essays have been attempts to use the psychotherapeutic perspective to illuminate the world in which we live.

However, the heart of psychotherapy is in the one-to-one encounter of the consulting room. This relationship is an adventure and a growth experience for both parties. Like all adventures it has its dangers, its longueurs and its moments of satisfaction and elation. No two journeys are the same and the outcome is always unpredictable. It requires from both patient and therapist commitment, doggedness and faith.

I hope that the following clinical material will give some flavour of how the work was for me.

The Silent Patient

I have a patient who has been sending me to sleep for years—or, to put it more accurately, in whose presence I regularly have to struggle against the tendency to drift into that area half-way between sleeping and waking.

I used to attribute it to post-prandial somnolence since we usually met after lunch, and to the long, long silences which make up most of every session. However, the occasional change of meeting time due to outside circumstances has had little effect on this tendency, so I have been forced to conclude that what I experience is in some way a transference phenomenon.

I wouldn't mind if the snatches of dream that I recall from such times told me something about him. They don't. They have little emotional charge and are boringly related to my own life. But woe betide me if I actually succumb to sleep; he notices and is hurt, although he had appeared totally withdrawn into his own inner world.

At one time, I thought nothing was taking place. Wrong! He made it clear the sessions were very important to him. At times I have felt

165

sadistically pinned down—with some justification. He needs me at the right distance. Too far, I am experienced as absent or possibly depressed. Too near, I readily become intrusive and he shuts up like a clam. But if I am content to wait, attentive but without expectation, something eventually emerges. I have occasionally accused him of blocking everything I try to do, and annihilating me in phantasy. I think there are times when this is true. At such times I experience irritation and anger in myself at his passivity. He has never been able to admit to what I believe is his passive aggression, but instead feels himself to be annihilated by my accusation, distressed, confused and unable to defend himself. Such incidents have been devastating for him. However, they no longer seem to occur. I still drift towards sleep.

Only recently have I been able to make sense of some of these phenomena in a way that is satisfying to him and to me, and which has freed us both.

(I understand from external sources that in his everyday life this man is experienced by others as caring and concerned, and functions well as a key member of his work team except when he is depressed. He came to see me originally because of his chronic, low-grade depression, and there has been no obvious sign of psychotic deterioration—rather a stubborn clinging to outside reality.)

In a recent session he began by talking about his former sister-in-law. She is a beautiful, vulnerable girl to whom sad and dreadful things have happened. Because of her high intelligence and a certain child-like appealing quality, it was a long time before my patient began to wonder if quite so many sad and terrible things could happen to any one person. He suddenly realised that all these events had occurred either before she came into the family, or when she was away from home, making any kind of confirmation virtually impossible. However, these recurrent and often bizarre happenings began to take place nearer home, making some kind of check possible. The result was a disturbing lack of correlation between the story as told, and the limits of reality surrounding the putative events.

The effect on my patient was dramatic. From being kindly and supportive beyond the call of familial duty, he became almost phobic about this girl. To talk about her caused enormous anxiety. A phone call or impending visit flooded him with fear. Actual contact with her resulted in paralysing depression and a desire to withdraw into nothingness which lasted for days. He felt, with some justification, that he didn't know if anything she said was true or not, or where, in all his acquaintance with her, reality lay.

He said that this was the same reaction that I had sometimes precipitated in him when I had accused him, falsely as he saw it, of some particular behaviour or feeling. He could never refute it, never tell me that I had got it wrong. He would feel totally confused and disorientated, and would withdraw into silent depression which would last the rest of the session and sometimes for days. I then had to wait until he chose to emerge—nothing I could do would winkle him out.

His next association was to some friends he and his wife had visited. They have a small child. (Although childless by choice, he has an acknowledged ability to comfort small children, and is very sensitive to any distress in them.) He recalled his excessive anger when one of the parents had said to this toddler, 'No, you don't want that, what you want is this … ' i.e. The parent had contradicted the child's expressed wish, and had substituted the parent's wish in its place in such a way that made it difficult for the child to protest.

I recalled his similar anger when, some time ago, his parents had visited them together with his sister and her family. At the meal table his nephew, when asked, had expressed a wish for bacon and egg for breakfast. Before anyone could respond, the child's grandmother (my patient's mother) had jumped in, 'No, you don't want that, you want ...' My patient, at the time, recalled how often that particular bit of family interaction had taken place when he was a child. On this occasion, his response was, 'Mother up to her usual tricks again!'—an uncharacteristically direct and aggressive statement for him.

In the next session, he was able to tell me at some length how afraid he was of becoming helpless and dependent on others' care, through illness or old age. We talked of his need to 'know everything about everything' so that he could be omnipotently self-sufficient.

He felt afraid that he was not functioning properly inside himself (talked about auto-immune disease—from a computer man!), and how frightening this is. He knew that at some level the unease was related to the fear of me not being there. He felt that he could not ask for help because he did not know where the discomfort was sited—only that he needed some kind of caring, and that it was before words.

He confessed that at times when he experienced this kind of anxiety, he would nibble his way through the larder and 'frig'. (I had not known of this.) He recalled too that when he is waiting while his wife prepares a meal, he is sometimes assailed by anxiety that she will become ill before the meal is ready, and then he will not be fed. (In practice, he is a competent cook and shares the cooking with her.)

This was the first session I have ever had with him in five years which I felt to be a truly analytic session. It marked a change in the quality of the work. He began to associate much more freely, and I became more alert.

A few days later he was able to tell me of a dilemma that has always been burdensome for him. It was something to do with having to accept what one is told even when there is no apparent sense in it, and it is contrary to one's own observation. The penalty of not accepting what one is told is to forfeit the relationship with the teller, or to become an outcast. The alternative was to try to sort out what in the telling was real from what was false. This involved holding a dual perspective on the world; but this was a very exhausting activity from which withdrawal into apathy was the only relief.

The connection with his mother was clear, as was much of his puzzling behaviour with me.

Perhaps I should add that this patient has clung to his relationship with me with great tenacity, feeling that there was something that needed sorting out with me, and in the face of my premature attempts to manipulate some sort of ending.

(1982)

This therapy extended over many years, and taught me much about counter-transference feelings and how to interpret them, since for long stretches of time they were my only source of insight into the patient's inner world. In retrospect, I am amazed, not that I sometimes got it wrong, but that I managed to get it right as often as I did!

The patient and his wife had opted to remain childless because he 'would not want any children of his to go through what he had had to!' I like to think that it was partly as the result of his therapy that they subsequently went on to have a family, and he proved to be a devoted and sensitive father.

Sadly, his early death in middle age, from natural causes, left me wondering about his ultimate viability.

An Interminable Therapy Terminated—
a contribution to the problem of the False
Memory Syndrome

A recent session with a patient left me feeling uncomfortable. I have known this patient over a period of many years. She has never been able to afford to come into therapy proper, as money has always been in very short supply. However, following our original group of sessions at a time of marital breakdown, she has continued to keep in touch with me. She has characteristically come to see me for a short run of weekly sessions during times of particular stress; and I feel she has made good use of me within those limitations.

She has a good depressive personality, and has struggled with considerable courage and ingenuity with her circumstances, and generally I can feel warmly disposed towards her.

She has been seeing me during this latest series of sessions for about six months, and has moved into an area of primitive experience and depth which I never expected to reach given the limitations under which we operate. (I think this has only become possible because her children have now left home, and she no longer feels the weight of her sole responsibility towards them.)

She arrived for this session looking very tired and distressed. She said she had had a sleepless night worrying about the prospect of a penurious old age. However, having briefly filled me in with the week's events she chose to lie on the couch and, instead of developing this train of thought, went immediately into a highly emotional state, sobbing, screaming, and expressing fear and distress in her body as she lay supine on her back. She didn't seem to know what this was about, and had no memories or associations she could connect with the experience she was acting-out.

As I sat quietly alongside, waiting for some kind of clarification to emerge, I found myself becoming increasingly irritated. The words 'histrionic', then 'hysterical' came into my mind. I found I was grumbling to myself, 'There's no need for all this fuss, whatever the reason!' I realised I was no longer feeling with her, but felt instead quite alienated. I recalled that when younger she was keen on amateur dramatics, and that more recently she had done some co-counselling, and I realised that I was having some distinctly ungenerous thoughts about both her and some of the alternative therapies on my doorstep!

She was able to offer some comment as a part of her observed her own behaviour. She wondered if she had been sexually abused since her pain seemed to belong in that part of her body, and she had a fantasy of a broom-handle being pushed into her vagina; but she also knew she had been reading about such a case in the press and perhaps that was influencing her thoughts.

The distress continued to the end of the session without any further clarification. I felt confused as to its meaning. I also felt atypically irritated and unsympathetic as she gathered herself together with difficulty to depart, as if I had been manipulated into playing a role I had not chosen.

These ungenerous thoughts recurred at intervals during the following day. At times I felt punitive, at others simply wished to be rid of her. I searched within myself for the sources of this upsurge of hostility, finding some, but nothing to justify the strength of the feelings.

Twenty-four hours later she telephoned me, sounding excited but more her usual self, and as I answered I felt my own feelings draining away. She felt she now understood what her distress was all about. It had triggered off a string of associations and connections which were still going on, and all sorts of things were falling into place. She would do her best to write it all down, and put me in the picture when she next saw me.

I felt somewhat concerned for her state of mind, since I had a sense that a mass of primary process material was flooding into consciousness. However, she had in the past managed much pain and distress in between her too infrequent sessions by just this means of writing it all down; and I felt I could trust her to contact me if she felt it was all becoming unmanageable.

However, I must confess to a certain sense of relief when she finally arrived a week later apparently well contained and in good spirits, and bursting to tell me her story. The episode she recalled, which had so distressed her the previous week was, she felt sure, a recollection of an infantile experience involving her mother. Because of the associations and connections which had emerged into consciousness, she was now convinced that as a baby she had suffered from a severe and intractable nappy rash. She felt that what she had experienced on the couch as a 'sexual assault' had been her mother's frantic and bad-tempered attempt to apply some soothing ointment to this protesting and uncooperative infant. The result, whether inadvertently through clumsiness, or intentionally 'for good measure' was that the ointment had also been applied internally causing a burning sensation.

She went on to make a series of connections to her behaviour in situations of intimacy, and particularly sexual intimacy, which we had worked over at length without ever fully resolving. (Although sexually attractive and able to excite the interest of potential partners, she was always aware of a lurking fear when real intimacy threatened, which subtly interfered with her heterosexual relationships. She had also had a repeated experience of getting close to a man and then being 'dropped' sometimes suddenly, sometimes by an inexplicable cooling-off. Although we had worked over these episodes in great detail, they kept recurring, to her increasing despair of ever finding another partner.)

There followed a great wealth of corroborative material which in effect brought together much of the material we had worked over through the years, and made sense of her vulnerability to some later life events. I was left in no doubt that this was a highly significant experience for her, that her 'memory' was indeed consonant with the temperament and behaviour of her (in many ways very good) mother, and I had a sense of having finally reached the climax of the work towards which we had struggled for so long, (although another part of me was prepared for the disillusion which seemed likely to follow!)

What was immediately important was the clarification of my hostile mood of that significant session. What was evoked in me appears to have been the feelings of the mother at that point—fed up to the back teeth with this screaming infant and the fuss it was making, at a loss as to how to manage it, and probably wishing it had never been born! (It was her first baby.)

(1992)

Post-script

In retrospect, it did indeed prove to be a turning-point and the beginning of a slow ending of this very lengthy relationship. Within the following two years, she gave up some of her idealised expectations of what therapy could achieve, and replaced them with more realistic goals. (A proper disillusion!) She found herself a sympathetic and patient man with whom she gradually developed an intimate and ongoing relationship. She also managed to find a job which moved her out of a somewhat sterile rut into a more creative environment; and she gradually weaned herself from her dependence on me, putting her energies into other activities.

As I look back, I feel I can now recognise that mixture of compulsive clinging together with equally compulsive distancing which operated in our relationship as much as in her other ones, and relate it to that 'assaulted' and fearful baby. Had it been possible to take her into therapy on a more frequent and regular basis, I am sure we could have reached this point sooner. However, it wasn't. It is a tribute to her persistence and faith that we did finally achieve it.

(1994)

P.P.S.

She asked for a session to help her make sense of something that had taken her by surprise, but which she was sure related to the area in which we had been working.

By this time she was well settled into a job which was more satisfying than her previous positions. Her relationship with her male friend had developed to the point where they had decided to think seriously about living together, and were engaged in working on their separate houses with a view to selling them and buying a joint property. While they had their occasional tensions, they had found a mechanism for talking about difficulties and resolving them.

She was now menopausal and had had no period for two years. It now seemed safe to discontinue contraceptive precautions—in her case, a Dutch cap. She was shocked to realise that the thought of not using her Dutch cap left her feeling extremely vulnerable. Rationally she knew it was nonsense, but the feelings were powerful and would not go away. She herself had no doubt that it related to that early infantile experience of intrusive penetration which had been re-enacted in my consulting room.

She went on to tell me of two minor incidents within the last few days which she felt were significant.

The first related to her partner. She had been renovating a piece of furniture with the intention of using it for the new joint home. When he first saw what she had accomplished, he made a remark which she heard as dismissive and down-putting. She immediately withdrew, feeling hurt. She did not expect that kind of reaction from him—he is usually a kindly and gentle soul. Is she making a terrible mistake as she did with her husband all those years ago? It was as if the relationship was totally ruptured.

Fortunately she recognised that she was over-reacting, and that she needed to put a stop to her emotional withdrawal. She told him of her feelings, they were able to talk about what had happened and the situation was resolved with minimal damage.

The second incident concerned her mother and her younger daughter, who had been living independently for some time. She was paying a rare visit home, and my patient P. took her to see her mother and step-father, expecting to give pleasure all round. However, the first reaction of P.'s mother to her grand-daughter, even before a proper greeting, was to comment unfavourably upon the clothes she was wearing. The incident was smoothed over at the time; but out of her grandmother's hearing, P's daughter confided to her mother that she was upset, that her grandmother had frequently upset her in this way in the past, and that this was one reason why she rarely visited. This was news to P. who was furious on her daughter's behalf, and subsequently confronted her mother about her behaviour. Typically, the mother attempted to deny what had happened, but P. took a firm line and obtained a grudging apology to the granddaughter.

P. said that such incidents had reminded her of times in the past when her mother had criticised her, undermining her confidence and self-esteem. In particular, there had been a recent, intense verbal tirade by her mother over the telephone on learning that P. and her partner intended living together. Her mother was totally opposed to this course of action, believing that marriage was the only acceptable option. P. felt that the suppressed anger provoked by this recent attack had added to her fury at the subsequent incident. It seemed to P. that such behaviour was the psychic equivalent of that very first 'attack' on her body-ego, evoking much the same sense of disintegration. P. had rarely been able to confront her mother successfully on her own behalf, but was at least able to do it now for her daughter.

Although the incidents were reported in the sequence given, in reality they occurred in reverse order. It seemed to me that the painful telephone conversation between P. and her mother had sensitised P. to anything resembling an unprovoked attack from a trusted figure, hence her 'over-reaction' to her partner's clumsy comment.

Although P. had really made the connections for herself, talking it out in my presence seemed to help objectify her inner reality and strengthen her sense of ego-boundaries. She is aware that she will need to watch her 'over-sensitivity' to criticism in her relationship with her partner.

(P. later said that she thought her reactions at this time were also fuelled by her anxiety at the prospect of greater intimacy with her partner, and the commitment of buying a joint home and living together.)

(1996)

P. has kept in touch with me over the years to the extent of a greetings card at Christmas and the occasional telephone call. She and her partner did indeed set up home together, and as far as I can tell have lived a contented and sociable domestic life since. Her children now have children of their own, and she has been surprised at how important this is for her. After such a long struggle as a single parent, she had had no enthusiasm at the prospect of becoming a grandparent. However, the reality is something else, and she now thoroughly enjoys spending time with them.

At a recent brief meeting she was looking attractive and well, appeared to be enjoying her life, and spontaneously commented that she no longer suffered from the bouts of depression which had dogged her in earlier times.

Our journey together extended over twenty years, and we each wondered at times if there would ever be any sort of satisfactory completion. Now, ten years on, we can look back with gratitude at our joint achievement.

(2006)

The Cannibal Gods

The acquittal of Kevin and Ian Maxwell [1] of the fraud charges brought against them led me to ponder on the difficulties of belonging to, and separating from, a dysfunctional family such as theirs. When a parent has such enormous and ruthless vitality, such a fluid sense of boundaries, and so little respect for the 'other', it seems as if the children have no reasonable choice but to either collude and remain within the fold, or to rebel and be forced to leave. If the latter, they then become demonised and 'beyond the pale'.

To the outsider, the choice facing the children seems an obvious one—to opt for flight and a separate life. In reality, too often the ones that get away appear to suffer as much, if differently, as those that stay.

The Maxwells are perhaps a particularly striking example of a family constellation that is far from rare. The classical Greek myth of the god Chronos who eats his own children is still acted out in our contemporary world.

There are mothers, too, who eat their own children. The Hindu goddess Kali and the pre-Christian Irish Brigid mythically embody this ferocious archetype. In practice, she is just as deadly as, if more stealthy than, her male counterpart. Incarnated as Aunt Ada Doom in *Cold Comfort Farm* we can laugh at her from a safe distance, but it is noteworthy that in that witty and perceptive tale, the author had to create an outsider to release the crippling hold the old lady had on her nearest and dearest. Stella Gibbons had clearly met the type.

A patient remarked to me recently that it was only since her mother died that she had begun to live. Her words echoed those made a few weeks earlier by another female patient some ten years her junior, and a similar sentence written last Christmas in his annual letter to me by a former male patient.

This first patient is now in her late fifties and came into therapy with me some four years ago, shortly after her mother's death. In case you picture some mousy worn-down creature, perhaps I should add that this particular patient presented as startlingly glamorous, and with a worldly self-assurance not often seen in my practice.

She has a long-term marriage to a man for whom she seems to have little affection or loyalty, and to whom she has denied sex for many years. There are no children but a lot of dogs, the care of which appears to be the cement which holds this relationship together. She has a social life of a rather superficial kind—coffee and shopping with girl-friends, a few long-term friendships with other couples. Her deepest relationships seem to be with other reformed alcoholics like herself with whom she has shared intensive group experiences over the years, and with the clients with whom she now works—alcohol and drug addicts. For these people she can express real affection and concern, and I suspect she is a very skilled addiction counsellor, simultaneously caring and confronting.

I feel she is very uninvolved with me, only coming because she must as a requirement of a further training commitment. I have supported her through several work-related crises as she has struggled to change careers, but have little sense that this has deepened our relationship. If she had a theme song, it would surely be *The Miller of Dee*. ('I care for nobody, no not I, and nobody cares for me!') I have indeed found it hard to care for her.

I can understand how she is as she is. As the younger of two daughters who were cared for by nannies, there seems to have been no one attachment figure in her early childhood, except her sister two years her senior. Mother was a very beautiful woman who enjoyed 'having a good time', and father was mostly absent (totally so for the six years of war). The two girls were sent away to boarding school when B. was three years old, and mostly farmed out to a nanny's relatives during school holidays.

When the father returned from the war, the mother abandoned the family group for two years, going off with her lover. On her return, there was an attempt to create a family unit and home, though the girls were still away at school. B. remained very attached to her sister, but the reciprocal relationship was deeply ambivalent and frequently destructive. (The sister appears to have become increasingly disturbed with the passage of years, and they now have little direct contact.)

I pieced together this story over a period of time, but such little affect as there was revolved around the sister. B. seemed to have little perspective on her mother's behaviour, and saw her father through the mother's eyes as 'useless'. Such negative feelings as B. expressed towards her mother derived from the adolescent years when B. hated to be expected to 'perform' for her mother's friends. The impression I had was of a highly narcissistic woman for whom children were just a nuisance, but who could relate to her adolescent daughters as self-objects as long as they fulfilled her expectations. At this stage B.'s need for her mother was such that she tried hard to be the sophisticated young woman that was demanded of her—looking beautiful, behaving beautifully— quaffing alcoholic drinks with the rest of the company.

At some point I realised that the woman I saw on my couch was B. still trying to be her mother's daughter, however much she overtly disowned her.

It was three plus years of this thin and unsatisfying relationship before B. began to really open up. I had earlier heard some of the details of the first marriage—an intensely emotional, boy-girl involvement, pre-nuptial sex, a back-street abortion and ensuing sterility, marriage and almost immediate flight by B. into wild promiscuity and heavy drinking, the enormous uncomprehending distress on both sides leading to divorce—but this story had been reported rather than felt. This time she brought her intense pain and regret for what she still felt had been her one true opportunity for happiness. Now she could see that her mother's disapproval of the marriage (as not good enough for her princess of a daughter) had hurt her deeply, but could not be faced and accepted. Her attempt to escape into an adult life had not succeeded; her compulsive need to remain her mother's daughter led her to act out in copy-cat behaviour of promiscuous sex and heavy drinking. Thirty years on, B. is at last truly grieving. The pain has been enormous, threatening a total loss of self and a descent into nothingness. The earlier resort to alcohol can be understood as an attempt to blot out the pain and the profound existential anxiety. This time she remained sober.

It was only after her mother's death that B. was able to set in motion the changes in her life—a different kind of work, and the training which is enabling her to make some positive use of her desperate history. It has required enormous courage just to survive much of her life, and perhaps it has been a sense of this which has enabled me to stay alongside until this point.

(Since that session, B.'s compulsive need to dress like a fashion plate—and beyond her means—has diminished. For the first time she has looked like the tired, middle-aged professional woman she actually is. She is still elegant, but she also feels real, and my sense is that she has at last shared something of profound significance with me.)

Her words echoed those made a few weeks earlier by another female patient of mine, whom I will call A. A. had approached me for therapy when in her mid-thirties and suffering from depression of a degree which seriously interfered with her life. The drugs prescribed by her G.P. after psychiatric consultation had brought little relief, and I was a last resort. I should not have taken her on— all the indications were against it. She had only come because she was sent, and it was clear from her manner that she resented having to come. She sat rigid and unbending, clothes, body, facial expression and speech all so tightly controlled that it was difficult to evoke information let alone an emotional response. My trial interpretations met with no reaction. The only positive indication was her concern for her children and the effect her illness might be having upon them. This single sign of a wish for change, and my respect for the source of referral, led me to take the plunge.

There followed years of once, then twice, a week therapy when I cursed myself for not following my intuition, such was the frustration of my work with her. She came regularly, sat on the edge of my couch as near the door as possible. She was always neatly dressed, her face devoid of make-up, her tiny bird-like figure uncomfortably close to anorexia. She gave so little of herself, it was hard even to know what really mattered to her. What she brought was mostly reportage, and my attempts to lure her into a transference relationship or something resembling analytical thinking seemed to get nowhere. Only occasionally did she allow herself to show distress, usually right at the end of the session as she dashed out through the door.

Several times in the first years I went into a session determined to bring the relationship to a close. When it came to the point I could never do it. Something somewhere made me feel that it would be a disaster for her if I withdrew. She, at some level, seemed to sense my intention because each time there followed some slight change in her. Slowly her story took shape, and slowly she allowed me to see her real feelings behind the highly controlled persona she presented.

What emerged was enormous rage, which not infrequently burst out within her nuclear family and frightened all of them. Her husband seemed to be a kindly man, concerned and patient, but his value system was such that he disapproved of overt aggression (as did she) and could make no sense of her outbursts. While forceful and assertive in his working life, he was apparently compliant and conciliatory with her, and unwilling to confront or quarrel.

She felt trapped in a lifestyle in which she was continually meeting others' needs while feeling that no one met hers, or indeed even recognised that she had any. She felt like the insubstantial shadow she so often resembled and, as she subsequently admitted, was on the edge of anorexia for extended periods of time.

Her history revealed an over-determined pattern. She was the elder of two children, and was conceived, so she was told, in order that her mother could avoid war-service. There were early feeding difficulties, father was often working away, and they had no settled home for the first few years of her life. Her brother was born when she was four years old and, as a sickly child, took up a great deal of the mother's time and attention. She felt dropped, of little importance in her mother's eyes, taking a lowly secondary place to the adored son. Fortunately, she had a good relationship with her father, but he wasn't always there for her.

Early schooling was disrupted by the circumstances of war (1939-45). Secondary education was at a convent school where again she was explicitly taught to be self-effacing and always to put others first. Her father was supportive in a quiet thoughtful way but would never stand up directly to his wife, seen as a powerful, controlling personality given to outbursts of temper and irrationality. (A. is aware that this is also a description of herself in a certain mood!)

A. learned to keep quiet, to evade her mother, to keep secret anything that was important to her. She privately determined to become a teacher, but this plan was greeted with fury by her mother who had no intention of her daughter leaving home, and belittled her capacity even to survive in the outside world. For once, A. stood her ground and escaped. It was indeed a difficult task for her to cope with the training; she seemed to evoke persecutory criticism from the occasional authority figure. However, she persisted and qualified, enjoyed the work and had no trouble keeping order in class. This was a good time.

The announcement of her engagement to a handsome young man brought a response akin to that of Sir Walter Elliot (in the 1996 TV adaptation of Jane Austen's *Persuasion)* on learning of his daughter Anne's betrothal, 'What, marry Anne? Whatever for?' (In the original novel the author characteristically communicates the same sentiment with greater subtlety, by innuendo.)

Sadly, an anatomical problem interfered with the establishment of an easy sexual relationship, and it was a couple of years before someone actually listened to A., performed a routine examination and addressed the problem. Conception was also difficult and only achieved after medical help. A. could not talk of her problems to anyone, and her husband H. saw them as 'women's stuff' which it was up to her to deal with. (The emotional damage was severe, and an easy sexual relationship was never established.)

A. nursed her terminally ill mother-in-law and went on trying to be a dutiful daughter to her own parents, but there were no reciprocal offers of help in baby-sitting, or support to enable the young parents to have time for themselves. The crunch point came at the time of the second baby's birth. A.'s brother finally rebelled against his dominant mother by contracting an 'inappropriate' marriage. The mother was beside herself with rage and distress, and discharged her feelings in all directions. A. was not spared the tirade; the fact that she had other more pressing responsibilities was totally ignored. Neither H. nor her father seemed willing or able to protect her. She felt there was no space for her to care for her baby, as the mother poured her feelings and demands down the telephone at all hours of the day and night.

A.'s depression began at this point. It became increasingly difficult for her to function in her chosen roles. She withdrew into the home, and meeting anyone outside was painfully difficult, to be avoided as much as possible.

Very slowly A. was able to tell me enough of this story for me to begin to piece it together. Every revelation tended to be followed by a retreat into a depressive mood in which she blamed her own inadequacies for her failure to cope with her life, as she saw it. Any comment of mine which could be heard as critical of those around her was met by protective denial of others' culpability, and increased self-persecution. It seemed almost impossible for her to move in any sense, so much so that I began to wonder if there was a psychotic core that was unassailable.

However, I did learn tangentially that life at home was easier. The children were growing up and, remarkably, seemed to be flourishing with little obvious disturbance.

Gradually A. seemed able to accept the perspective on her life that I was offering her, but was still unable to change anything. She could not assert her own needs in a constructive fashion, and I had a powerful sense that it suited everyone else that she stayed as she was. I, too, seemed to be trapped into metaphorically pumping ship to avoid her total collapse.

For me, relief came when her husband's job disappeared, and the ensuing financial constraints led her to cease therapy. It was her decision, made very firmly to me, and it felt appropriate to accept it whatever my private misgivings.

She returned spontaneously a year later to resume the sessions. That intervening year had been difficult for her husband with the loss of his work and income, but she was able to be supportive and encouraging, and he eventually found another job, albeit working away from home for much of the week. Her ability to be of help to him during this time, and to think clearly and constructively at a time when he was confused and lost had done much for her self-esteem, as had her capacity to manage the home and children in his absence

The other major change during this year was that her mother, who had developed cancer some years previously, was now entering the final phase of her illness. Characteristically A. proved a tower of strength during this time, particularly in supporting her father as he nursed his wife, and subsequently during the mourning period.

Life began to change for A. She took some time out from individual therapy to join a therapeutic group—a very brave step for her! She made a friend, and found she had things to offer the group. She became more socially outgoing. Her dress became subtly more lively—a bright scarf, some long earrings.

She began to train for some voluntary work, and asked for my ongoing support as she struggled with its demands. I was frequently impressed by her powers of observation, the subtlety of her intuitive understanding, her courage in confronting situations which terrified her. She survived a lengthy and demanding course and went forward for assessment—at the last possible moment, such were her anxieties!

To her own surprise, she is now well into the work and a valued member of the group, allowing herself to move into new experiences as they are offered her. She still shrinks from being judged, but can cope with constructive criticism, and has been able (albeit with great trepidation) to assert her own needs as to who and what she finds helpful.

The children have all achieved university education and appear to be managing their lives with skill. They are somewhat ambivalent about their mother's new work, since she is no longer always immediately available for them, but she accepts my suggestion that perhaps they need to feel that she has her own life in order to feel happy about leaving her. Her husband is somewhat bewildered by the changes; his home is no longer so immaculate, and his personal servant less reliable. Both are wondering how it will be when the youngest flies the nest. A. alternates between resigned acceptance of the lack of real intimacy, and anger with him for his refusal to engage. She no longer takes all the blame, but is aware that her past behaviour has contributed to the stalemate, and that she still has her own difficulties in this area.

A marked feature of this case was the patient's massive denial of her negative feelings which then became turned against herself, hence the depression. However, there was more to the depression than this. It became apparent that when the weight of evidence was reflected back to her so that her customary defence mechanism of denial could no longer be maintained, far from this lifting her mood, it became imbued by another and more dangerous quality. The fear seemed to be that of depersonalisation, of losing herself entirely, of sinking so far that she could never get back; and the anxiety was intense. At these points a psychotic breakdown felt uncomfortably close.

It seemed that the real danger was of an inner world without objects. If she allowed herself to experience the anger and rage she actually felt towards those closest to her, the power of her feelings would destroy her internal objects, and indeed her entire inner world. Far better for her to see everything as her own fault, the result of her own inadequacies, than to let go the idealisation of others, make contact with her rage and risk catastrophe.

I think, too, that as a small child she had been very frightened by her mother's rage. I suspect that those outbursts had imploded through A.'s defences leaving her temporarily disorientated and acutely vulnerable. That vulnerability towards her mother remained; she tried to keep her defences intact against such onslaughts—in vain. They still occurred and they still devastated her.

Why did she not get right away? She had done it once when she went to college. One factor was that although she could, I think, have abandoned her mother, (there seemed little in the relationship that was positive); what she could not do was abandon her father. That relationship had been vital to her psychic survival as a child, and was still very important to her. She was temperamentally very like him, and he did much in his relationships with his grandchildren to fill the gaps left by her husband's work-related absences. Also, and importantly, she felt he needed her in order to survive life with his wife, and subsequently without her.

The other factor pinning her down was her husband's temperament and value system. It seemed as important to him to see himself as a 'good boy' and a 'good son' as for her to be a dutiful daughter. He tended to put everyone else's needs before those of his immediate family, thus disguising his own fear of intimacy. He too had had a mother with a temperament similar to that of his mother-in-law, which he had survived by massive denial. Fearful of confrontation, he was always quick to deny A.'s reality. I suspect it suited him all too well for her to carry his depression as well as her own.

Joan Raphael-Leff has some telling comments on the quality of 'stuckness' so marked in the case of A. She talks of the experience of some young people whose 'parental needs eclipse awareness of their own'; 'of undefined passive waiting for one day when they will be fed/rescued/played with/compensated for past deprivation.' She talks of how 'the same individual may oscillate between both stances of passive waiting and active altruism' ... and of how 'the inertia of the first stance and the sacrificial endurance of the second promote stuckness in life and an inability to move on.' She could be describing A!

Why did the death of A.'s mother produce such marked and rapid change? I think that as the mother's health declined, she became less critical and explosive, and less frightening. Also, during the illness A. felt she had something to offer and could make reparation for her now conscious hostility. After the death, A. felt safe enough to recall the positive aspects of her mother, her vitality, her intelligence, that drive which could have been used so much more creatively in more favourable circumstances.

Also, by this time, the work we had done together had had its effect even if it was not easy to discern! A. was able to tell me that she felt she had had an experience of good mothering from me, of how for long periods it was only the regularity of our sessions that had enabled her to get through the week, and that it was my hope and persistence that had helped her cling on when part of her was close to suicide. She also added that she hoped she never had clients like herself! (She is now able to demonstrate a nice sense of humour!)

M.'s dysfunctional family had some things in common with those already discussed—a narcissistic, controlling, deeply disturbed (probably borderline) mother, who did not want this last child; a mostly absent father, well-meaning but unable to confront and deal with his wife. M. managed to find (just about) enough good objects in her life to arrive at late adolescence with some hope intact. She separated off in no uncertain manner by leaving her country of origin to settle in one which she had visited, and on which she projected her idealised expectations. If the cultural transition was difficult, she nonetheless survived it, found supportive friends, found herself a husband. What she had not anticipated was her parents leaving her. Both died with little warning within a short time of each other, without any real reconciliation having taken place.

Circumstances, including the needs of small children, combined to make the work of mourning difficult—or perhaps it was the other way round. There was something so devastating about this double blow that perhaps it was necessary to cling to the mundane demands of life in order to keep going, to prevent the malignant regression that threatened. This only surfaced later when someone (the therapist) appeared on the scene to contain her, and to think that which for her was unthinkable. (M. used denial in some ways similar to B.)

M. like A. had married a man who resembled her mother rather than her father. Though their sexual relationship had been an active one, there had always been difficulties for her in engaging, and it could at times feel abusive to her (since she was really looking for a parental quality of loving). Difficulties increased as the therapy took hold, the therapist took on the maternal projections, and regression deepened. The sado-masochistic aspect of the marital relationship became increasingly apparent and M., after many months of somatising her pain to a degree which frightened her (and myself in the counter-transference), finally separated from her husband.

Since then M. has struggled with enormous real-life problems, but has survived and grown. She has acquired a higher degree, a professional qualification and a capacity for self-assertion when needed. She is still lacking a deep self-confidence and is quickly undermined, at which point a disintegrating panic threatens. I have a sense that the deaths of her parents were experienced as retribution for her act of defiance in leaving them, and that her good internal objects are readily attacked by these vengeful internal persecutors. As with A., from time to time she does evoke persecutory behaviour from others.

She has not yet found herself another mate which saddens her, and she is aware of her envy on this issue. Her experience of benign parental couples is thin, and she has little confidence in her ability to make a new relationship work. The good news is that she has been able to retrieve the positive aspects of her father, and to understand and achieve some forgiveness for her mother. It has helped that on the infrequent occasions when she meets with her siblings, they can share their memories and perceptions of how difficult life at home actually was. This injection of shared reality eases the pain and protects M. from the internal persecution of her own retroflected destructiveness.

For all three of these patients, the struggle to achieve a life that feels real has needed enormous courage, and at times it is as if they have clung to life by their fingernails. Each one has feared that they might not survive, and suicide has beckoned.

I am concerned at the way this depth of struggle is somatised in this kind of family. All three families have a high rate of death from cancer. I worry for these individuals (though all are healthy at present), and ponder on the putative connection.

These are cases of destructive mother-daughter relationships. What of the other parent-child combinations—mother-son, father-son, father-daughter?

Tom was someone who made very good use of me during a relatively brief therapy. Mid-fifties, a highly intelligent and successful professional man, married with adult children, he had become involved in an extra-marital affair in a manic attempt, I believe, to avoid an incipient depression. When that affair was terminated abruptly by the woman, he plunged into a black depression which brought him to see me.

His family of origin consisted of an elder sister, a shadowy father, and a mother very like A.'s—dominant, controlling, endlessly complaining and paranoid when thwarted. His childhood had been very limited and constricted by her regime—there was little contact with other families—but he was an able child which pleased her, he received support from his teachers to reach university, and opted to make his professional career at the opposite side of the country. Meanwhile his sister married and emigrated!

Even at fifty-odd, he dreaded his occasional duty visits to his mother which routinely evoked depression in him. He experienced her as full of complaints and bitterness, interminably trying to evoke guilt in those she thought should be looking after her. She had always hated Tom's wife and took no interest in her grandchildren. Tom's reaction to her was near-phobic.

What became apparent during therapy was the link between his current depression and sense of disintegration, which came close to destroying his world, and the depressions of childhood—the rejection because he couldn't or wouldn't do what was demanded, and the sense of worthlessness and isolation that followed.

His mid-life crisis I understood as the breakdown of his false persona—mother's boy, the successful conventional professional man—in part triggered by enormous and extended pressures at work (which he had successfully managed.) I saw the affair as an abortive attempt to find something more real and alive. He went through a phase of middle-aged hippiedom, left his job, went travelling abroad, played with various notions of an alternative life-style. His wife too was changing and went into therapy. Fortunately the marriage held, he found a number of off-beat activities which made good use of his professional skills, and has gradually returned to his work but in a format which feels right and comfortable for him.

He keeps in touch to the extent of a letter at Christmas. In the last one he wrote 'Life has been so much better since my mother's death two years ago.' He goes on to say that all is well with the family, that they are thoroughly enjoying being grandparents, and that work is giving him pleasure again.

R.'s father was a Maxwell figure—an expansive, sociable man, a pillar of the local business community, he occupied a lot of space in every sense. He was, I believe, very controlling and bullying at home. I think this, not because of what R. told me—indeed there was much defensive idealisation of both parents—but because of the way that R. himself behaved towards his step-children and, to a lesser extent, his own sons. The contrast between this aspect of his behaviour and the mild-mannered and intuitive man I met in the consulting room was stark. However, he had a strong sense that a man should be 'master in his own house', and while this in part derived from the sub-culture in which he was reared, it was undoubtedly built upon an identification with his father.

Both parents had, I felt, a real pride in their only child and his achievements—but his father compulsively tried to manage his son's development in ways that were often inappropriate. For instance, he insisted on R. joining the local golf club and playing with his own potentially influential friends. It was on one such occasion that R. experienced a curious episode in which the outside world suddenly felt unreal, he himself felt unreal, and what he described as 'the veils' came down between himself and the outside world. A doctor was called who prescribed two weeks bed-rest and sedatives, but the veils never lifted and were one of R.'s presenting symptoms some fifteen years later.

Just prior to this episode, newly-qualified in his profession, he had been working in a busy London firm headed by a man he described as much like his father—demanding much and providing little real support. R.s escape from home into work, which had served him well throughout his adolescence, had ultimately failed. At that point he had what I believe to be an acute psychotic episode.

This combination of high expectations and bullying demands, but with no real support, was crucial. R. recalled during therapy how, as a child, he had longed for real intimacy with his father, but he could recall only one occasion when he experienced it—doing a bit of car maintenance together. He had had an adolescent fantasy, which still persisted, of being the lead singer in a pop group. The all-important part of the fantasy was the backing group—the supportive group he felt he had never had.

Where was his mother in all this? She was described by R. in terms which suggested a somewhat immature woman, compliant and dependent. She had the sole care of her son during the first two years of his life as father was away in the army, but I felt that she was not able to give R. much sense of his own separate identity during that time. Rather, he had the impossible task of trying to fulfil *her* dependent needs—and, as an adult, R. had a part of himself that was a compulsive carer. Father, on return from the army, turned him out of his mother's bed and instituting a harsh domestic regime, destroying what little foundation he had as a basis for growth, He reacted with an illness which required temporary hospitalisation, with its accompanying separation from mother.

The adult R. was hypochondriac, was driven by a mild but distressing fetish, and masochistic sexual fantasies which contained his painful unmet needs.

At first sight D. seemed to have little in common with my previous examples. An intelligent and handsome professional woman in early middle age, she had already had some valued therapy, and was curious about the psychoanalytic perspective. She approached me because she felt she was still not on as good terms with herself as she should be.

She felt she had done all the work she needed on her family of origin, but instead brought material around recurrent and often violent marital rows, and her ongoing battles with her children. It soon became apparent that she was engaged in a perpetual power struggle on both these fronts, and was nearly always the loser. She could only engage in sexual activity with her husband after he had defeated her, while with her children she was alternately demanding and indulgent.

When not engaged in battle, she was lethargic and depressed. She was continually trying to make time for her own activities in the family schedule, but when she had time on her own she was unable to use it creatively, and was overwhelmed by a sense of emptiness and lack of motivation.

She suffered from a series of ill-defined but disabling maladies, and was constantly seeking help from a variety of alternative practitioners while very wary of orthodox medicine. She was extremely resistant to my attempts to give meaning to her symptoms, as also to my interpretation of her pattern of flight from intimacy, and from dependency on any one source of help.

She felt that, as a professional woman, she should be a calm and mature dispenser of wisdom, always unruffled and in control of herself. The contrast between her ego-ideal and the reality of someone who had great difficulty in managing an explosive temper was very painful to her. She was obsessed with her physical symptomatology, but seemed unable to use anything I offered her in the way of interpretation. She spent much of her sessions drifting away into a world of her own. I had no sense of my having any significance for her, and there was no continuity between sessions. In spite of my ongoing efforts to engage with her, I could form no coherent narrative out of what she brought, and I had no sense of any change in her life. However, she continued to come.

What I gradually formulated out of my counter-transference was a sense of primitive regression to an infancy in which there was nobody there for long stretches of time. Her mother was a woman who cared for her children in a brisk, problem-solving mode, but who had little capacity for empathy (and had herself had an emotionally deprived childhood). D. had done her best to be self-sufficient, but the effort left her exhausted and plagued by hypochondriacal aches and pains. (I think, in fact, that she used her physical dis-ease to maintain some sense of identity and embodiment as an infant.) She tried hard to use her considerable intelligence in a creative way, had brief bursts of enthusiasm and activity which soon faded, and was frequently paralysed by her sense of abandonment.

I realised that she had at some point in her young life given up hope that her mother could give her what she needed, and had turned to her father for her emotional supplies. This had appeared to work very well. She was the most academic of her siblings, the 'boy' her father wanted to follow in his footsteps (her brother being dismissed by him as 'mediocre'). In her teens, she accompanied him to the professional meetings he attended, and went on to study his own subject at university. She was seen as a 'success'.

However, throughout the adolescent years, her 'success' came to be felt as increasingly hollow to herself, and after graduation she chose to move in another direction. At this point her father dropped her, showing little further interest in her development, although for a time she made a considerable success in her chosen field. She drifted into a series of brief relationships, all with older married men, dropped out of her high-powered lifestyle for a few months, then had a brief episode of breakdown which terrified her. It was at this point that she met her husband and allowed herself to be persuaded into marriage despite the difficulties posed by their different backgrounds. Her father was openly disappointed in her, and rarely came to visit her. Neither parent showed much interest in her babies or in her subsequent career.

I came to realise that D.'s previous therapies had indeed helped her to dissolve the close bond which had tied her to her father. However, she was then thrown back on the relationship with her mother. That emotionally bleak early relationship had been followed by one in which she was constantly nagged and controlled by a mother who had outbursts of furious temper, just like D. herself. Moreover, D.'s mother was a despised and denigrated figure within the family, so that D. could gain no sense of her own value as a wife and mother by identifying with her. D. felt herself to be very masculine (not my perception) and hated her appearance accordingly (her father's boy), yet felt driven to relate to her husband as a rival rather than a sexual partner much of the time.

D. still has little sense of who she really is. She cannot safely identify with either parental figure. Her sexual identity is confused, and she would really like to escape from her painful body and live on another, more ethereal plane. However, I feel that her physical symptoms are necessary to her in order to anchor her in her body, and in the real embodied world.

D.'s father was not a grossly disturbed man, although he did manifest some schizoid and narcissistic traits. The damage suffered by D. was so great because of the inadequate foundations of her personality in the very early years.

Theoretical issues

Now let me try briefly to put this multiplicity of phenomena into some kind of conceptual framework.

- I am describing a number of patients, each of whom was the child of a narcissistic parent and was significantly damaged by that experience. These patients were themselves narcissistic in varying degrees—only in A. and M. was it was very well hidden beneath a depressive persona, where it formed the core of the resistance with which I struggled for so long.

- The role of the other parent is significant. He or she tends to be absent or rather inadequate. In my experience, narcissistic personalities tend to marry spouses who allow themselves to be dominated or marginalised. In my two cases of damaging fathers, the mothers had already failed their child because of their own problems. I can think, too, of examples where potentially good-enough mothers have had their role, and their self-esteem in that role, undermined by a narcissistic husband who could not bear to share his wife's attention, even with his own child. In the case of A. her father was able to provide something positive when he was around, and this was the source of such strength as she had.

- All these patients, at the time of entering therapy, were trapped in relationships which had a distinctly sado-masochistic cast, except for Tom whose passionate affair nevertheless had something of this quality. Two of them, R. and D., had overt and highly-developed perverse fantasies which were continually on the verge of being acted-out. In both these cases, the child had at an unconscious level become the parent's sexual object—R. as a boy was his mother's 'little man', and openly preferred to his father; D. was taken around as her father's consort.

There are a number of factors which are widely accepted as contributing to the development of the narcissistic personality.

Several of these are present in the life-history of these children of narcissists.

a) Mirroring

All have suffered from a failure of accurate mirroring in the formative years. This concept will be familiar from the work of both Winnicott and Kohut.

Robbins argues that 'the mother is neither responsive to, nor encouraging of, the infant's need signals and initiatives, but instead imposes an agenda consisting of her own fantasy attributions'. The mother responds to the infant's need signals with devaluation and disapproval. This leads to an active internalisation of the maternal devaluation. As a result 'the infant is left without a reliable autonomous perceptual apparatus, without the rudiments of instinctual development, without dependable instincts. He has only a shared illusion to cling to'.

Gear, Hill & Liendo suggest that: ' ... if the mother and father fail to recognise the desire of the infant, but instead induce in it the complement of their own unconscious and repressed desire ... the child is educated to be a mirror and to find others who will in turn mirror its own repressed unconscious desire.'

b) Perversion of authority.

Gear, Hill & Liendo contend that in the normal situation authority defines rules, and then rewards a child for compliance or punishes it for rebellion. However, beyond insisting on these rules, authority recognises the child's separate identity. Within these rules, the child can develop an autonomous sphere, and gradually develop a relationship of equality with the other.

The alternative mode as found in these families prevents this normal resolution, and perpetuates an asymmetrical relationship of dominance and submission. The figure who is responsible for exercising authority on behalf of the culture either uses this position to assert omnipotent control over the child, or else surrenders it to the child. In such a situation authority remains unmediated by the values of the culture it is supposed to transmit, and is simply exercised for its own sake. The child can then adopt either a masochistic or a sadistic position, but no other. The psychic possibilities are grossly restricted.

c) Envy

I see this as having a central role in these case histories.

Each of these narcissistic parents was highly controlling, resistant to the efforts of the child to separate, and envious of any signs of autonomy and creativity. Each of these children had, out of their need for a good parent, attempted a false solution by identifying with the aggressor.

All had felt immensely hurt by what they experienced (accurately) as envious attacks on their creative selves. These attacks plunged them into a state of disintegration which felt unbearable. In the end, it was as if each one of them could only survive by actively destroying those bits of themselves which evoked these envious and destructive attacks. It was as if, as children, they could not face the reality of being dependent on someone who at some level wanted to crush the life out of them. The need to have a good parent was so strong that they would sooner destroy those aspects of themselves which evoked such attacks.

A. had fought a good fight, and was only slowly ground down into the desperately rigid and inhibited (and stubborn!) wraith I first met. The continuing attacks from her mother led to reciprocal attacks by A. upon herself as she tried ever more desperately to be a good dutiful girl, and came ever closer to breakdown. R.'s history is similar.

The Jungian analyst Nathan Schwarz-Salant argues that the narcissistic character has generally been subject to massive envious attack in childhood. In an effort to avoid a repetition, he or she 'hides his prize from others and from himself.'

'Narcissistic characters have generally experienced a chronic lack of mirroring often stemming from parental envy. When parents lack a sense of their own identity they become sensitive to how their children like them, or how it adds or detracts from their sense of esteem. Not only will they be unable to mirror the child's emerging personality, but they will want to be mirrored by the child, who feels this keenly. Often the child feels it has something special the parents want, yet the specialness must be subverted to mirroring the parents, to giving back the responses that make the parents feel secure. Otherwise there will be an uncomfortable feeling in the environment, a disquiet due to the parents' discomfort with their child's uniqueness. This undertone is the working of envy, the spoiling effect stemming from the parents' insecurity and jealousy of their own children who may create an identity they themselves lack. The end result of this process is that rather than feel itself loved and accepted, the child feels hated.'

It is against this feeling of being envied and hated that the narcissistic character erects defences. The child retreats to a masochistic position because this is felt to be safer. The self is suppressed and, in identification with parental attitudes, is hated.

d) Failure to negotiate the oedipal position

Central to the development of these patients is the failure to progress from the dyadic mother-child relationship to the triangular oedipal position. This leaves the boundaries and sense of self unclear. The child is uncertain about his origins and place in the scheme of things. An ever-present threat will be the loss of differentiation of self due to the fusion of self and other. The response to this threat engenders an oscillation between the danger of fusion on the one hand and isolation on the other, bringing with it a proneness to shame and self-consciousness.

A crucial factor determining the failure to enter the oedipal position may be the mother's wish to denigrate the role of father. The malignant alliance between the mother's omnipotent wish to do without the father, and the child's desire to remain close to mother and exclude father may trap the child in a developmental cul-de-sac.

With the exception of Tom none of these patients had been able to establish a satisfactory sexual relationship. The over-riding developmental task has been around the difficulty of establishing a

198

good internalised mother. A. established a good relationship with her father, but it has been as a nurturing parent rather than a sexually exciting man. Insofar as A. felt herself part of an oedipal triangle, her mother was too frightening a figure (and father ultimately too passive) for it to be satisfactorily resolved.

None have had a good parental couple inside them. In each case the child related to the two parents as two separate and often warring individuals.

A. R. & D. have all, to some degree, suffered from a failure to internalise what Dana Birksted-Breen has called 'the symbolic function of the penis-as-link', representing both the separateness and link between self and other and between internal objects, as opposed to fusion versus fragmentation. This structuring is necessary in order to create mental space and the capacity to think. All have felt over-whelmed by their experiences and feelings, and have needed external help to construct anything resembling a coherent narrative. (Fonagy, 1991)

For all of these patients, the struggle to achieve a life that feels real has needed enormous courage, and at times it is as if they have clung to life by their fingertips. Each one has feared that they might not survive, and suicide has beckoned.

Kohut writes: 'There is something very frightening as an adult .... when there is a sense of not fulfilling one's basic program. We realise that there is a nuclear program in an individual—a tension arc between early ambitions and early ideals via a matrix of particular skills—that points into the future and points to a particular fulfilment. Once the program is in place, then something clicks and we have a degree of autonomy; this degree of autonomy we call the self. It becomes a centre of independent initiative that points to a future and has a destiny. It also has its own natural, unfeared decline and end.'

There seem to be a number of general issues raised by these cases.

1. One is the long-term effect on children when they are emotionally misused (abused?) in order to boost the

parent's vulnerable ego. How can they grow up if the parent cannot grow up enough to let them separate?

2. Secondly, how does a child manage to obtain its basic emotional supplies from a parent who has them to offer, if inconsistently, but is too dangerous to be trustworthy? For years, A. was adept at keeping me at just the right distance —close enough to be nurturing, not so close as to be threatening. The real needs were well hidden, and the defences high. It could be said that A. was stealing what she needed from me, since there was so little mutuality between us. Certainly my counter-transference feelings at times supported such an interpretation, but it did not feel appropriate to verbalise them.

    a. I have had similar feelings in my work with R. and D.

    b. It was only during the revision of this paper that the author became aware of the work of Mervin Glasser on these issues. His delineation of the universal challenge of mother-child separation as a Core Complex is a concise and illuminating theoretical construct, and would have been very helpful to her thinking! His two papers indexed below discuss many of the points touched on in this essay.

3. Thirdly, these cases brings to mind the well-supported concept that a bad object is better than no object at all. It is surely this which traps children within a dysfunctional and downright damaging family constellation even after they are old enough to escape. For the infant, to destroy the mother is to destroy life itself. For the mother to refuse permission for the child to separate, to differentiate and become its own person, is to deny it a life that is experientially real. It is a kind of theft. It is the goddess eating her children.

4. There is a broad issue here as to how certain patterns of psycho-pathology are transmitted down the generations, how and to what extent they can be modified, and what

factors are involved in that modification. Lily Pincus [2] and Christopher Dare addressed this issue in their stimulating book *Secrets in the Family*. Perhaps because so few of us have their extensive experience of working with families, concentrating as we do on individual therapy, I feel there is much still to be understood in this field.

The Therapeutic Task

I would suggest that the chief aims of the therapeutic task are, in brief:

- The replacement of pseudo self-sufficiency by an entering into relationship, and an admission of dependency needs. The author has found helpful the technique of mirroring, as suggested by Kohut, in order to facilitate the development of a relationship.
- The need for the idealisation of the parents to be dissolved and mourned.
- Modification of the internalised persecutor.
- The relinquishing of the false self—the grandiose self— leading to an acceptance of a more real sense of self.

Inevitably, given the history of this kind of patient, therapy tends to be a long and slow. Change can only be risked as trust is developed, and there will be much testing out of a hidden nature.

Notes

[1] Robert Maxwell was a powerful figure in the world of publishing and business in the latter years of the twentieth century. At the time of his mysterious death by drowning he was under police investigation, accused of raiding the pension funds of his businesses to hide financial losses. Subsequently his sons Kevin and Ian were put on trial, and Kevin was declared bankrupt. Although it was never altogether clear to what extent the sons had been involved in his activities, Robert was known to be such a bully in his relationships, always threatening and aggressive if opposed, that there was some public sympathy for their dilemma. The daughter had escaped the family net by making a separate life for herself in the USA.

[2] Lily Pincus was one of the many German-Jewish immigrants who came to enrich our cultural life as the result of the upheavals in Europe in the mid-twentieth century. A social worker by profession, she was a founder member of the Institute of Marital Studies at the Tavistock Institute, and collaborated in writing a number of publications in this field. Her book *Death and the Family* is an insightful study of the effect of bereavement on family relationships.

(1997)

References

Austen J. (1818) *Persuasion*.

Bettelheim B. (1992) *Recollections & Reflections*. Penguin.

Birksted-Breen D. (1996) 'Phallus, penis & mental space.' *International Journal of Psychoanalysis (IJPA)* **77**, pt.4

Bleger J. (1967). 'Psychoanalysis of the psychoanalytic frame.' *IJPA*, **48**: p.511-519

Blue L. (1979) *A Backdoor to Heaven* p. 16. Fount (Harper Collins).

Bollas C. (1987) *The Shadow of the Object: Psychoanalysis of the Unthought Known*. Free Association Books. London.

Bowlby J.A. (1988) *A Secure Base: Clinical Applications of Attachment Theory*. Karnac.

Canter D. (1994). *Criminal Shadows*. Harper Collins.

Carroll L. (1871) *Alice Through the Looking Glas.s*

Chasseguet-Smirgel J. (1985) *Creativity & Perversion*. Free Association.

Cooper J. & Maxwell N. eds.(1995) *Narcissistic Wounds*. Whurr Publishers Ltd.

Euripides (406 B.C.) *The Bacchae*.

Fonagy P. (1991) 'Thinking about thinking'. *IJPA* **72** 4 pp.639-656

Fox R. (1989) *The Search for Society: Quest for a Biosocial Science & Morality*. Rutgers University Press, New Brunswick & London.

Freud S. (1960) *Standard Edition*. Hogarth Press.

— (1900) *The Interpretation of Dreams*

— (1901) *The Psychopathology of Everyday Life*

— (1913) *Totem and Taboo*

Gear, Hill & Liendo (1981) *Working Through Narcissism: Treating Its Sado-Masochistic Structure.* New York: Aronson.

Gibbons S. (1932) *Cold Comfort Farm.* Longmans, Green & Co.

Glasser M. (1992) 'Problems in the psychoanalysis of certain narcissistic disorders' *IJPA* **73** pp.493-504

Haldane J.B.S. (1927) *Possible Worlds & other papers.* Essay Index Reprints 1991.

Hardy A. (1979) *The Spiritual Nature of Man.* The Alister Hardy Society.

Holmes J. (1993) *John Bowlby & Attachment Theory.* Karnac.

Isherwood C. (1935) *Mr. Norris Changes Trains.* Rpt as *The Last of Mr. Norris.* New York: New Directions 1945.

Julian of Norwich (1980) 'He keeps all that is made' from *Enfolded in Love.* Darton, Longman & Todd.

Kandel E.R. (1999) Biology & the future of psychoanalysis. *Am. J. Psychiatry* **156** pp. 505-24

Kaplan L. J. (1991) *Female Perversion.* Penguin.

Kauffman S. (1995) *At Home in the Universe.* Viking / Penguin. London.

Khan M. Masud R.(1979) *Alienation in Perversions.* Hogarth.

KohutH. (1971) *The Analysis of the Self.* New York: International Universities Press.

— (1972) 'Thoughts on narcissism and narcissistic rage' in *The Search for the Self: Selected Writings,* vol.4 :1968-1981. ed. Paul Ornstein. Karnac. 1991.

Laing R.D. & Esterson A. (1965) *Sanity, Madness & the Family.* Tavistock. 2nd edition: Karnac. 1970.

Lake F. with Root H. & Demant V.A. (1966) *We Must Love One Another or Die*. Hodder & Stoughton.

— (1981) *Tight Corners in Pastoral Counselling* Darton, Longman and Todd.

Leibniz G.W. von (1714) *Discourse on Metaphysics & the Monadology*. trans. George R. Montgomery 1992.

Leigh R. 'Panel Report on Perversion' in *Barcelona Congress 1979 of the IPA. IJPA* **79**, pt. 6.

Mancia M. (2006) 'Implicit memory & early unrepressed unconscious.' *IJPA* **87**, pt.1

Mandelbrot B.B. (1977) *The Fractal Geometry of Nature*. Freeman. New York.

Mas S.A. (1992) 'Ambiguity as the route to shame.' *IJPA*, **73** p. 329-339.

Masterson J. F. (1978) *Psychotherapy of the Borderline Adult*. Brunner/Mazel. New York.

Mollon P. (1993) *The Fragile Self.* Whurr Publishers Ltd.

Moorehouse G. (1997) *Sun Dancing*. Weidenfeld & Nicolson.

Ogden T.H. (1989) *The Primitive Edge of Experience*. Jason Aronson Inc.

Pincus L. (1976) *Death and the Family*. Faber.

— & Dare C. (1978) *Secrets in the Family*. Pantheon Books, New York.

Piontelli A. (1992) *From Foetus to Child*. Tavistock/Routledge.

Raphael-Leff J. 'Narcissistic displacements in childbearing' in Cooper & Maxwell (1995) above.

Robbins M. (1982) 'Narcissistic personality as a symbiotic character disorder'. *IJPA* **63** 457-473.

Rose S. (1992) *The Making of Memory; From Molecules to Mind*. Bantam. London.

Rosen I. 'Perversion as a regulator of self-esteem' in *Sexual Deviation* (1979) ed. I. Rosen. Oxford University Press.

Schwarz-Salant N. (1982) *Narcissism & Character Transformation.* Toronto: Inner City Books.

Searles H.F. (1986) *Collected Papers On Schizophrenia.* Karnac.

— (1986) *Countertransference & Related Subjects. Selected papers.* Karnac.

— (1994) *My Work with Borderline Patients.* Karnac.

Segal H. (1995) *Psychoanalysis, Literature & War.* Karnac.

Shah I. *Tales of the Dervishes* (1967): Jonathan Cape.

Socarides C.W. (1988) *The Pre-Oedipal Origin & Psychoanalytical Therapy of Sexual Perversions.* International Universities Press Inc.

Stapledon O. (1948). 'Interplanetary Man' *Journal of the British Interplanetary Society* **7**, 6.

Stevens A. & Price, J. (1996) *Evolutionary Psychiatry.* Routledge.

Stoller R. (reprinted 1986) *Perversion: The Erotic Form of Hatred.* Maresfield Library.

Symington N. (1993) *Narcissism: a new theory.* Karnac.

Teilhard de Chardin. (1970) *Let Me Explain.* Collins Fontana.

Vaughan H. (1621 – 1695) *The Morning Watch.*

Williams H.A. (1965) *The True Wilderness.* Constable.

— (1972) *The True Resurrection.* Mitchell Beazley.

Winnicott D.W. (1971) *Playing & Reality.* London: Tavistock.

Index